MW00710350

Navigating Detours on the Road to Success

A LAWYER'S GUIDE TO CAREER MANAGEMENT

by

Kathleen Brady

INKWATER
PRESS

Portland • Oregon

www.inkwaterpress.com

ISBN 1-59299-138-6

Publisher: Inkwater Press

Printed in the U.S.A.

To the graduating class of 1989 at Fordham University School of Law. For me, it all began with you....

ACKNOWLEDGMENTS

Behind every successful endeavor, there is a cadre of people who contribute in ways both big and small. As someone who practices what she preaches, I always reach out to my own Board of Advisors for advice, information and input. Never has that been more true than in the creation of *Navigating Detours on the Road to Success.* Many of my friends and colleagues offered ideas and suggestions that have been incorporated into the book. Of course, a few people stand out above the masses for their extraordinary support.

Gail Parker, Merna Skinner, and **Phylis** and **Hank Behar** are among my most trusted advisors. Spend ten minutes with them and you will walk away not only inspired to reach your dreams, but with 50 practical suggestions as to how to go about it.

Input from my sisters, **Joanne Brady** and **Renee Brady Capone,** also helped shape this publication. Joanne provided much needed administrative support and Renee provided candid "consumer" reactions to ensure the publication was reader friendly.

Finally, my friends **Gihan Fernando,** Assistant Dean of Career Services at Georgetown University Law Center, and **Bonnie Hurry,** Director of Recruiting and Legal Staff Services at Davis Polk & Wardwell and 2005-6 President of the National Association for Law Placement. Given their expertise, they offer perspective on current trends and realities in the legal marketplace. But they do so much more than that. Gihan and Bonnie can always be counted on to support my efforts and to candidly (sometimes brutally!!) provide the feedback I seek. They are my friends and confidants. Thank you for reviewing the manuscript, for always sharing your wisdom and for being such great pals.

Table of Contents

Navigating Detours on the Road to Success

CHAPTER ONE

The Road to Success Is ALWAYS Under Construction

The road to success is paved with detours, roadblocks, speed bumps and potholes. The average American will work for 10 employers, keeping each *job* 3.6 years, and change *careers* 3 times before retiring. Sometimes the change will be voluntary; sometimes the change will be instigated by outside forces. Either way, change is inevitable. Therefore, if you want to get the most out of your career and maximize your chances for professional development, you have to expect and prepare for multiple transitions as you travel along the road to success.

A transition does not only mean a job change. Morphing from a junior associate to a mid-level associate, or associate to partner, is a transition; so is switching practice groups or offices, or going from a full-time to a part-time schedule. Then there are also the transitions in other areas of life that will impact your career path. Consider the impact becoming a new spouse or parent could have on your career, or the death of a parent or an unexpected illness or a change in the economy. Learn to navigate the terrain and you'll not only reach your destination faster, you will also enjoy the journey.

Most people experience transitions as something that happens TO them rather than as something they can plan for and control. They arrive at career/life decisions not on the basis of any meaningful thought process, but rather on familial obligations or societal expectations. And then they wonder why they are unhappy and unfulfilled.

If you are like most people, you spend more time planning your vacations than you do planning your career or your life. Consider the vacation planning process. Most of us choose a destination based on specific criteria about how we enjoy

spending our time. Why not use the same mindset as a first step towards mapping out a career/life strategy? Think about what you like to do and where the best place to do it might be. Invest time and effort to assess your skills and knowledges as well as your wants and needs and you can fully integrate your professional and personal selves to achieve success.

You have the power to create the career—and the life—you want as long as you are willing to accept that transitions are inevitable and develop a strategy to deal them. Learn to control the things you can and develop strategies to cope with those you cannot.

Balance Professional and Personal Identities to Maximize "SUCCESS"

Think about success for a minute. What does it look like? Odds are, every person reading this has a different answer. However, there are four common elements in every vision of success. They are:

1) being content about your life;
2) achieving measurable accomplishments that compare favorably to others with similar goals;
3) believing that you have a positive impact on people you care about most;
4) leaving a legacy in order to help others experience future success.

Each element contributes to the way you experience success **right now**. Success is NOT a future event or something to aspire towards. Think of it as a current state of being: the ability to pay full and undivided attention to what matters most in your life at any given moment.

Of course, the difficult part is figuring out what matters most.

That's where self-assessment comes in. Most lawyers fail to engage in the self-assessment process. At best, they can assess their lifestyles—where and how they want to live, what their immediate needs are, and what their needs are likely to be tomorrow. These are certainly important considerations, but evaluating lifestyles is no substitution for self-assessment. You must also decide how you want to use your skills and talents. How do you want to invest your "human capital" to achieve the desired return on your investment? To answer that question, you MUST be able to articulate your Abilities (skills, accomplishments and special knowledges), Beliefs (motivations, passions, values, goals and ideals) and Conduct (action plan, work style and temperament). These are the ABCs of career management, and while they are influenced by environment, heredity and even spirituality, they are ultimately controlled by you. Once you learn how to identify your Abilities, harness your Beliefs and Conduct yourself in a positive, can-do manner, you will be able to create an internal definition of success and enjoy the career—and life—you have designed.

Career theorists have examined a multitude of variables that influence career choice at different points throughout the life cycle and remind us that career planning is a continuous process of choices and adjustments. Career planning is not about having a rigid, well-delineated path mapped out; it is about learning to position yourself to be prepared to react to changing circumstances that are inevitable through the course of your life. By anticipating transition points, you can develop effective strategies to manage them.

Studies suggest that during your twenties and early thirties, you are likely to:

- commit to an occupation, lifestyle, spouse;
- focus on "establishing" yourself within your chosen profession;
- concentrate on your career "advancement," with a vision toward the future.

Typically, the career trajectory during this phase is a steep incline with well-defined benchmarks to assess growth.

Sometime during your late thirties and early forties, you are likely to:

- discover your choices are no longer rewarding;
- experience a "period of crisis" as the result of some life-altering event (death of a parent, birth of a child, divorce, etc.)
- become more specific about your needs, focusing on the here and now;
- reassess your choices;
- accept your current situation or opt for change.

The trajectory during this stage is less steep and in some instances even flat. At this stage you have proven what you can do and now you are deciding if you still **want** to do it. For some, this period provides an opportunity to reap the benefits of years of hard work; they allow their careers to operate on automatic pilot while they tend to other facets of their life. For others, it is a time of discontentment and frustration as they try to determine what lies ahead.

By the time you reach your late forties and early fifties, most people are old enough to have acquired considerable life experience and to have learned from it, yet young enough to act on it and make the necessary course corrections by readjusting goals and shifting priorities. People may opt to change careers, change lifestyles or change both. They may also opt to do nothing. Recognize that opting to do nothing is a choice too.

Transition may be brought on by a major event, disenchantment with current choices, recognition of more satisfying possibilities, etc., at any stage. While you may not be able to control the event, you can strengthen your coping strategies to respond effectively to them. Don't view such changes or course corrections as a sign of weakness or as a lack of commitment. Rather, see them as a prerequisite to personal and professional growth.

By considering where you are professionally in the context of your lifecycle, you can begin to assess where you are at currently, where life is likely to take you in the future, and how to map out a focused but flexible career path that allows you to navigate any detours or roadblocks you may encounter.

EXERCISE: Reflections

To help you get started with the self-assessment process, consider your responses to the following questions. Jot down your responses. Note any patterns, themes and inconsistencies. These are not easy questions. Take time to truly think about them.

1) How do you **describe your current job/career** to others?

2) At the **start of your career**, what were your ambitions/long-range goals?

3) Thinking about your **first real job**, why did you make that choice? What were you looking for and how did it advance/contribute to the achievement of your ambitions/long-range goals?

4) Consider your **first job change**. How did it come about? Who initiated the change? What were the reasons for the change? How did you feel about it? What impact did the change have on your ambitions/long-range goals? (Repeat this question for each additional job change.)

5) Reflecting upon your career to date, can you identify times when change seemed more than routine? What **life event(s)** served as the catalyst(s) for change? How did you feel about it? What impact did the change(s) have on your ambitions/long-range goals?

6) Are there periods of your career/life that stand out as particularly **happy/enjoyable times**? What made them enjoyable?

7) Are there periods in your career/life that stand out as particularly **unhappy/difficult times**? What made them unhappy/difficult?

8) What **messages** did you receive about work during your formative years?

9) What did your **parents/significant adults in your life do for a living**? What were their views towards work?

10) What did your **parents/significant adults in your life want you to do** for a living?

11) What do your **siblings do** for a living? What are their views towards work?

12) If you **are struggling** to make a career/life decision, can you describe **why**?

13) **Have your goals changed** since you started your career? When? Why?

14) How do you see your **career/life progressing** over the next decade?

15) Without worrying about qualifications, education, salary, security, etc., describe your "**fantasy" job/career**.

BONUS QUESTION: **Why** do you work?

Getting Started: The ABCs of Career Management— Abilities, Beliefs, Conduct

The five-step career planning process outline described below provides a frame for designing an individualized career path that will enable you to design a professional life that enhances your personal life.

Abilities

Step 1: Focus on your skills, strengths, assets and talents, not your shortcomings.

The best strategy to direct the course of your career is to identify your skills and talents. (The exercises in Chapter Two will help you assess your abilities.) You must be able to articulate what you can do and what you know. While you want to be aware of any shortcomings you may possess, you do not want them to dictate your path and prevent you from following your dreams.

Beliefs

Step 2: Know what you TRULY want.

Take some time to think about what you *really* want to do. Do not underestimate the power of passion. The world is filled with examples of people who achieved their goals—against all odds—because of their passion. Consider Neil Perry, the San Jose football player whose right leg was amputated below the knee after a horrific injury in a game during the 2000 season. Hours after his leg was removed, Parry vowed he'd play football again, an unlikely proposition under the circumstances. Yet, in September 2003, Parry was back on the field and fans were hard pressed to notice a difference between his abilities and those of his two-legged teammates. He had the drive and passion to withstand 25 operations and countless hours of rehabilitation and physical therapy to achieve his goal. If you allow yourself to be fueled by your internal drive instead of any external pressures, your shortcomings will have little or no impact on your ability to succeed. They may present hurdles, but your passion will galvanize your skills, strengths and talents so you can easily clear the bar.

Neil Perry is but one example: With passion, that combination of forces of mind, will, resources and heart, we can move mountains. Exercises in Chapter Two will help you clarify your beliefs.

Step 3: Do not accept conventional wisdom unconditionally.

There will always be some perfectly logical reason why your qualifications are insufficient for a specific position. Anticipate what those reasons might be and decide for yourself if they are, indeed, insurmountable, or merely a hurdle to clear. Remember, conventional wisdom would suggest that amputees can not play football. Passion is stronger than conventional wisdom. **Excellence always trumps stereotypes and perceptions.** Always strive to be the exception to the rule. Do your homework so that you know what the conventional wisdom is and then plan a strategy to deal with it. Chapter Four will provide you with tips on how to stay abreast of workplace realities so you will always be in the know.

Conduct

Step 4: Develop an action plan (SET GOALS).
Think about the direction you'd like your life to take. What do you want to accomplish during your lifetime? During the next five years? The next year? Think about what you need to do to make it happen. You will be amazed at what you can accomplish when you are clear about what you want and have an action plan in place to guide you. Chapter Two will provide you with the tools you'll need to set and achieve your goals.

Step 5: Make course corrections.
Keep in mind that goals and motives may shift as you mature and grow. What moves you to action today may bore you and disillusion you tomorrow. Change should not be seen as a sign of weakness or as a lack of commitment. Change is a strength that allows people to adapt to ever changing circumstances. Chapters Six through Ten outline specific steps to take when a course correction is needed.

Summary

Managing your career development is an on-going process that includes planning and strategizing based on information about yourself and the world of work, the match between them and the actions you take. You must make a lifelong commitment to actively manage your career/life and learn to adapt to the inevitable transitions you are destined to encounter.

Finding the courage to forge your own path and construct a personal definition of success in the face of external obligations and pressures isn't easy. In fact, it is downright scary. Do it anyway. I promise, once you get started you will find the process is more affirming than it is scary. Take a deep breath and take the first step. The rewards will be monumental.

CHAPTER TWO

Learn to Drive

Identify Your Abilities, Beliefs and Conduct

Learn Your ABCs

In Chapter One we discussed how important it is to be able to articulate your **A**bilities (skills, accomplishments and special knowledges), **B**eliefs (motivations, passions, values, goals and ideals) and **C**onduct (action plan, work style and temperament). When you feel confident in your abilities and are convinced that you deserve to be successful, little will stop you from achieving your goals. The exercises in this chapter provide the tools to do just that.

The best strategy for directing the course of your career is to focus on your skills. Jobs are joint ventures in problem solving. The idea is to find a match between an employer's needs and your skills. It is important to constantly assess:

- What needs to be done?
- What can <u>you</u> do?

Let's start by identifying what <u>you</u> can do.

EXERCISE: What Can You DO?

STEP 1: Review the following skills and indicate the extent to which you believe you possess each ability on a scale of 1 to 5. (1 = Very Little... 5 = Very Strong)

I have the ability to:

Accept responsibilities	1	2	3	4	5
Adapt to change	1	2	3	4	5
Adhere to deadlines	1	2	3	4	5
Analyze data	1	2	3	4	5
Apply legal principles	1	2	3	4	5

Assemble deals	1	2	3	4	5
Assimilate new data quickly	1	2	3	4	5
Be responsive, reliable and conscientious	1	2	3	4	5
Be self-directed	1	2	3	4	5
Build internal/external networks	1	2	3	4	5
Collaborate with colleagues	1	2	3	4	5
Communicate well orally and in writing	1	2	3	4	5
Compete	1	2	3	4	5
Conceptualize	1	2	3	4	5
Conduct legal research	1	2	3	4	5
Confront	1	2	3	4	5
"Connect the dots"	1	2	3	4	5
Counsel/advise clients	1	2	3	4	5
Decide/act in pressure situations	1	2	3	4	5
Delegate	1	2	3	4	5
Demonstrate commitment	1	2	3	4	5
Demonstrate good judgment/common sense	1	2	3	4	5
Demonstrate political judgment	1	2	3	4	5
Develop business	1	2	3	4	5
Develop rapport and trust	1	2	3	4	5
Digest large quantities of material	1	2	3	4	5
Draft documents	1	2	3	4	5
Edit	1	2	3	4	5
Empathize	1	2	3	4	5
Explain complicated ideas in simple terms	1	2	3	4	5
Facilitate	1	2	3	4	5
Follow through	1	2	3	4	5
Formulate strategy	1	2	3	4	5
Gather facts	1	2	3	4	5
Initiate	1	2	3	4	5
Inspire confidence	1	2	3	4	5
Interview	1	2	3	4	5

Keep confidences	1	2	3	4	5
Lead	1	2	3	4	5
Listen critically	1	2	3	4	5
Maintain "systems"	1	2	3	4	5
Manage complex tasks	1	2	3	4	5
Manage details	1	2	3	4	5
Manage people	1	2	3	4	5
Mediate	1	2	3	4	5
Motivate	1	2	3	4	5
Negotiate	1	2	3	4	5
Organize	1	2	3	4	5
Persuade/promote/sell	1	2	3	4	5
Predict/forecast trends	1	2	3	4	5
Prioritize	1	2	3	4	5
Produce quality work	1	2	3	4	5
Put in long hours	1	2	3	4	5
"Read" people	1	2	3	4	5
Research	1	2	3	4	5
Resolve conflicts	1	2	3	4	5
Retain information	1	2	3	4	5
Schedule deadlines, set goals	1	2	3	4	5
See "big picture"	1	2	3	4	5
Solve problems creatively	1	2	3	4	5
Speak persuasively	1	2	3	4	5
Strategize	1	2	3	4	5
Summarize	1	2	3	4	5
Supervise	1	2	3	4	5
Synthesis	1	2	3	4	5
Take risks	1	2	3	4	5
Theorize	1	2	3	4	5
Tolerate delays/wait	1	2	3	4	5
Train/teach	1	2	3	4	5

Troubleshoot	1	2	3	4	5
Understand objectives and work standards	1	2	3	4	5
Use technology proficiently	1	2	3	4	5
Work well under pressure	1	2	3	4	5
Work efficiently	1	2	3	4	5
Write persuasively	1	2	3	4	5
Write technically	1	2	3	4	5

STEP 2: For each characteristic you ranked 5, go back and add the phrase "for example," and provide a specific example or story illustrating when you used that skill well. You will be able to use these stories to illustrate your ability to take on a desired assignment or demonstrate to an interviewer that you are the ideal candidate for a job.

> *Example: I have the ability to organize. For example, I organized a job fair coordinating 200 employers, and 900 students from 14 different law schools. My job was to make sure that every student was in the proper place every 20 minutes and that the employers had the correct resumes.*

STEP 3: For those skills you ranked 1 or 2 consider whether you:

A: NEED to develop this skill further to achieve your goals. If so, determine what action steps you must take.

B: WANT to develop this skill further. If you don't want to and you don't believe you need to in order to achieve your goals, don't worry about it.

EXERCISE: Identify Your SUCCESS Patterns

Transferable/functional skills are ways that we characteristically react to problematic situations throughout life. As a child, if confronted with a puzzle or task, your reaction may have been to organize the pieces and then examine alternative solutions. As a teenager repairing a car engine, the same problem-solving skills may have been utilized. These problem-solving skills are known as "success patterns" and tend to become set during the teenage years. Over the years, we tend to become more proficient in the use of our favorite skills, but because they seem innate, we do not always recognize them as marketable skills.

To help you identify your success patterns and marketable skills, list 10-12 achievements or accomplishments from throughout your lifetime. Include those related to work, leisure and education. An accomplishment can be something big like closing a complicated deal, winning a jury verdict or landing a big client. Or, it can be something very simple, like receiving an A on a school project or hosting a surprise birthday party for a friend or managing a personal crisis. Your skill patterns will emerge no matter which accomplishments you select. Consider dividing your life into segments to ensure you cover the entire spectrum of your life (i.e., "High School, College, Law School, Job #1" or "Teens, 20s, 30s, 40s" etc.) Review billing records and look through yearbooks and family photo albums to help jog your memory. You may not be able to complete this exercise in one sitting. Consider doing it over the course of a few days, adding accomplishments as they occur to you.

ACHIEVEMENTS STEP 1: Define the segments of your life and then list a total of 10 accomplishments, with representation from each segment.

	Segment 1	Segment 2	Segment 3	Segment 4
a.				
b.				
c.				
d.				
e.				

STEP 2: Select three or four accomplishments on your list that you would like to examine more closely. Write a paragraph detailing every step you took to make this event happen. Concentrate on HOW you did it, but do

not analyze. Have fun with this—do not worry about grammar, spelling or punctuation. At the end, note how you felt at the conclusion of the event.

Samples

#1 In the fourth grade, every student had to do a presentation on a specific country. I was assigned Guatemala. I went to Funk & Wagner encyclopedia to do my research on the population, climate, etc. I also went to the library and took out all the books I could find on that country to ensure I knew all there was to know about Guatemala. I copied information onto index cards and organized the cards into categories. Unlike my classmates, I was excited about standing in front of my classmates and showing off how much I knew. My teacher told me I did a good job and gave me an A+. I felt proud.

#2 In senior year of college, I took an elective course that required an oral presentation at the end of the semester. Because the course was in my major, I was well versed in the subject matter and not overly concerned about the presentation. The day before the presentation, I spent about 15 minutes organizing my thoughts. The following day in class, another student asked if she could deliver her presentation first because she was very nervous and wanted to "get it over with." She had handouts and diagrams, and despite how prepared she was, she appeared flustered and unorganized. When it was my turn, I walked to the front of the classroom with my half page of notes feeling slightly worried that I did not have all the supporting documentation she had. But I delivered my presentation— barely referring to my notes—in an interesting and engaging way. The audience applauded and I received an A. (They didn't applaud for my classmate and she only got a B.) I remember feeling surprised at how easy it was and feeling slightly superior to my classmate who had clearly invested more time in preparing than I had.

#3 I am extremely proud of having my non-fiction book published. I spent several months researching the topic, drafting the chapters and putting the information together in a way I believed would be useful to the reader. A friend of a friend presented the draft to a small, independent publisher who agreed to publish it. In order to boost sales, I scheduled several presentations on local TV & radio shows, Barnes & Noble bookstores, etc. The publisher printed twice as many copies as he expected and told me how pleased he was to find an author who wrote well and who enjoyed the marketing component of the book business.

From the sample stories, one might assume that the author enjoys being recognized as an expert and has an innate ability as a public speaker. The author demonstrated research and writing skills as well as presentation skills. This information is important to know and easy to translate to employers during the interview process. ("Ever since the fourth grade, I knew I enjoyed researching topics and was comfortable speaking in public. Those skills will serve me well as a trial lawyer.")

Your Achievement Stories

Achievement 1:

_____

_____

_____

_____

_____

Achievement 2:

_____

_____

_____

_____

Achievement 3:

_____

_____

_____

_____

_____

Achievement 4:

_____

_____

_____

_____

_____

STEP 3: Review your stories, circling all skills mentioned. Read the stories aloud to a friend or colleague and ask them to note the skills they heard. (This is a great way to learn how you are perceived by others.) Note any themes and patterns.

What Do You WANT to Do?

People tend to be motivated by what they *like*, not by what makes sense. Yet, they allow "what makes sense" to pull them in a direction they'd rather not go, which ultimately leads to burnout or unhappiness. For example, once the investment in law school has been made, many lawyers feel enormous pressure to seek employment that offers the highest financial return, usually in the private sector. And, as more financial responsibilities accumulate—mortgages, children's' educations, etc.—hopes and desires of public service, politics, lawyering for the poor and unfortunate and the like tend to wither as efficiency and economics point in only one direction. But remember, balance between professional and personal goals is the objective. By tapping into what you *like*—your passions and motives—you can energize your career development and enrich your life.

Internal motives combine the forces of **mind, will, resources and heart**. When you are truly motivated you have the **MENTAL STAMINA** to focus and concentrate no matter what is happening in the world around you. Sheer **WILL** provides the necessary drive and determination, commitment and dedication, as well as discipline, persistence and endurance to achieve your goals in the face of seemingly insurmountable obstacles. Motivation enables you to capitalize on your internal **RESOURCES** such as your skills, talents and abilities as well as strategize how to use external resources to your advantage. But most importantly, motivations capture the forces of the **HEART** and fuel your efforts through enthusiasm, excitement, and passions. When your heart is committed, NOTHING can deter you.

Success is a subjective perception based on what YOU as an individual value. Values are those intangible principles and standards that bring meaning to your work and motivate your involvement and commitment. You need to ask yourself what your values are and which hold the most meaning and importance to you. People tend to feel most comfortable when surrounded by others who hold similar values and in situations where their values are appreciated. The following exercise will help you further identify career/work values and factors crucial to your job satisfaction.

EXERCISE: Identify Your Values

Step One: Rate the importance of each item.
A = VERY IMPORTANT   B = IMPORTANT   C = NOT IMPORTANT

___ Achievement	___ Education
___ Advancement	___ Effectiveness
___ Aesthetics	___ Emotional Growth
___ Affiliation	___ Ethics
___ Altruism	___ Excellence
___ Authority & Power	___ Excitement & Adventure
___ Autonomy	___ Fairness
___ Being Needed	___ Family
___ Boss You Respect	___ Flexibility
___ Challenge	___ Focus
___ Change	___ Fringe Benefits
___ Closure	___ Friends
___ Commitment to Goal(s)	___ Harmony
___ Competition	___ Health/Physical Fitness
___ Complexity	___ High Profile
___ Control	___ High Risk/High Reward
___ Courage	___ Holistic Approach
___ Creativity	___ Honesty
___ Direct Impact	___ Improving the World
___ Discovering New Things	___ Independence
___ Diversity	___ Individuality
___ Economic Return	___ Influencing People

___ Innovation   ___ Religious Observance

___ Integrity   ___ Respect

___ Intellectual Stimulation   ___ Responsibility

___ Interesting Work   ___ Routine

___ Job Security   ___ Salary

___ Justice   ___ Social Relevance

___ Knowledge   ___ Specialization

___ Leadership of Others   ___ Stability

___ Leisure Time   ___ Status

___ Lifestyle Integration   ___ Structured Environment

___ Mentoring   ___ Supervision

___ Morality   ___ Supervision of Others

___ Physical Appearance   ___ Training

___ Physical Environment   ___ Traveling

___ Pleasure   ___ Upward Mobility

___ Popularity   ___ Variety

___ Power   ___ Working Alone

___ Recognition   ___ Working on Teams

___ Relationships   ___ Other_____

Step Two: Rank the A's on a scale of 1-10 with 1 being the MOST important and 10 being the least important. Refer back to this list whenever you are confronted with transition decisions.

EXERCISE: Identify Your Career Core

As people accumulate work experience, they begin to make choices about how to best meet their needs and balance their career/life goals. From these choices they begin to acknowledge what is most important. Up until that point, people may have a vague sense of their talents, motives and values, but it is only when confronted with difficult choices that dominant themes emerge. When all needs cannot be met, it is important to know which one has the highest priority. That priority can be defined as the "career core," a combination of perceived areas of competence, motives and values that you would not give up. Core personal values do not change, but priorities can be challenged in complex situations. Career cores serve as an anchor and shape the choices we ultimately make.

STEP ONE: Consider each of the eight endings to the following phrases and rank order them according to which completed sentence is most like you. The ending most like you should be ranked 8, the one next most like you 7 and so on with the one least like you ranked 1.

1. My ultimate career goal is:

   a) to be recognized as an expert in my field _____

   b) to manage people and processes _____

   c) to be autonomous _____

   d) to obtain financial and employment security _____

   e) to start my own business _____

   f) to make the world a better place _____

   g) to be constantly challenged _____

   h) to achieve life/work balance _____

2. For me to feel satisfied in my career, I must have a job that allows me to:

   a) develop technical skills to the highest level of competence _____

   b) lead an organization, making decisions that affect many _____

   c) have complete autonomy and freedom _____

   d) be financially secure _____

   e) own my own business _____

   f) serve the community _____

   g) solve "unsolvable" problems _____

   h) work to live not live to work _____

3. I would rather stay in my current position than accept a promotion that would:

   a) take me away from my area of expertise _____

   b) eliminate my managerial responsibilities _____

   c) restrict my autonomy and freedom _____

   d) jeopardize my security _____

e) limit my creative input ____

f) undermine my ability to be of service to others ____

g) be too easy ____

h) compromise my ability to pursue outside interests ____

4. I will be "successful" when I:

a) am recognized as an expert in my field ____

b) manage the careers of others ____

c) am in a position to define my own tasks, schedules and procedures ____

d) feel secure ____

e) can unleash my creative energies ____

f) help those in need ____

g) feel challenged ____

h) have a life ____

STEP TWO: Add 5 points to the highest ranked ending for each of the four phrases.

STEP THREE: Total points for each letter response. Circle your highest score.

Total: a____ b____ c____ d____ e____ f____ g____ h____

Research suggests that most people can be described in terms of 8 "self-concepts" or "career cores." The career core can shift or lie dormant as we pass through different life stages, but ultimately, the career core is tied to our self-image. This short test was designed to help you to identify the one thing you would NOT give up if forced to make a choice.

Total

____A   **TECHNICAL COMPETENCE**
People who scored highest in this category are drawn to the *content* of the work. They develop a technical expertise and commit themselves to a life of specialization. Most people begin their careers by specializing as a means to climb the ladder of success, achieve security, branch out on their own, etc. However,

those with a TECHNICAL COMPETENCE CORE are motivated by the need to be a recognized expert in their field. They measure success through "external equity", comparing their salaries and responsibilities to others at comparable organizations with comparable skills. They will tolerate administrative and management tasks, but are irritated by general managers who impose directives despite their limited expertise.

_____B   **MANAGERIAL COMPETENCE**

People who scored highest in this category view specialization as a trap. They want to know enough about several functions within the business/industry to be able to move up the ladder of success. They develop analytical competencies that enable them to identify problems/solutions cross-functionally and they develop strong interpersonal skills in order to influence, supervise, lead and manage others within the organization. They measure success through "internal equity," comparing their compensation to those above and below them within the hierarchy, and seek promotions that would elevate compensation and responsibilities.

_____C   **AUTONOMY**

People whose career core is AUTONOMY have an overriding need to do things their own way. They like clearly delineated, time-bound assignments within their area of expertise, but they want complete control regarding how to complete the assignment. Autonomously driven people measure success in terms of merit pay for performance and they seek promotions that provide them with greater autonomy.

_____D   **SECURITY**

Those who scored highest in this category organize their careers so they feel safe and secure. They focus on the *context* of the work, preferring future events to be predictable so they can relax in the knowledge that they have "made it." They prefer jobs/careers with tenure and good retirement plans. They identify with the organization, no matter what level of position. They measure success in terms of continued employment.

_____E   **CREATIVITY**

People in this category have an overriding need to "create" a new business, product or service or "reshape" existing ones to meet their own specifications. This need stems from the desire to prove it can be done as a result of *their* expertise, talents and motivations. The driving force is not money, nor even challenge, but ultimate "ownership" of the creation.

_____F   **SERVICE**

Those who score the highest in SERVICE are oriented more by values than actual talents or competencies. Their motivation is dedication to a cause. They define success as the ability to serve/ help others.

_____G   **CHALLENGE**

These people build their careers around conquering the 'unconquerable." Success is derived from overcoming obstacles, solving "unsolvable" problems or winning out over an extremely tough opponent. To feel successful, people in this category must be able to consistently exercise a competitive skill.

_____H   **LIFE/WORK BALANCE**

For these people work is important and satisfying only if it can be successfully integrated in their lifestyle. Success is measured in terms of flexibility to achieve work goals within a context of limiting interference with personal/family needs.

Goal Setting

Career planning is like solving a business problem. Every successful business venture begins with a comprehensive business plan, updated annually, outlining goals and objectives. Such plans are designed to be flexible in order to accommodate unexpected market changes and opportunities. Likewise, you need to have a focused but flexible comprehensive career plan.

EXERCISE: Develop Your Action Plan

First, list the 10 to 12 most important things you want to accomplish during your lifetime. Date your list. These are your **LIFETIME GOALS.** From that list, select the 4 or 5 things you want to accomplish in the next 5 years to create your **5-YEAR PLAN.** Then, review your 5-year plan and choose the 3 or 4 things you want to accomplish during the coming year. These are your **ANNUAL GOALS**. For each **ANNUAL GOAL** listed, write down the answer to the following questions.

1) WHAT is the goal?

2) WHY do I want to achieve this goal?

3) WHEN will I achieve this goal?

4) HOW will I achieve this goal? (Or: *What 3 things do I need to DO?*)

5) WHO can help me achieve this goal?

Repeat this process once a year, referring back to your LIFETIME GOALS and 5-YEAR PLAN. Revise each list as circumstances warrant. Once you are clear about what you want and have an action plan in place to guide you, it will be easy to accomplish your goals.

LIFETIME GOALS   Today's Date _____

List the 10-12 important things you want to accomplish during your lifetime.

1. _____

2. _____

3. _____

4. _____

5. _____

6. _____

7. _____

8. _____

9. _____

10. _____

5-YEAR PLAN GOALS   Today's Date _____

List in order of priority the 5 most important things you want to accomplish in the next 5 years.

1. _____

2. _____

3. _____

4. _____

5. _____

ANNUAL GOALS   Today's Date _____

List in order of priority the 3 most important things you want to accomplish during the coming year.

1. _____

2. _____

3. _____

Complete one Action Plan Worksheet for each goal listed above.

ACTION PLAN WORKSHEET

My **goal*** is to:

_____

I want to achieve this goal **because**:

_____

I want to achieve this goal **by (date)**:

_____

The first three things I must **do** to achieve this goal are:

a) _____

b) _____

c) _____

People who can help me achieve this goal include:

a) _____

b) _____

c) _____

* Remember, goals must be S.M.A.R.T: **S**pecific, **M**easurable, **A**ttainable, **R**elevant, **T**ime-bound.

Summary

It is important to consider the competencies and personal qualities you want to live by and see reflected in the workplace. Value your unique gifts and talents and you will, in turn, be valued by others. Catalogue your skills, abilities and special knowledges continually and be prepared to tell people about them. Don't think of it as shameless self-promotion; instead think of it as sharing relevant information with people who can help you achieve your goals.

CHAPTER THREE

Ace The Road Test

Display Appropriate Workplace Behaviors

Project Reliability, Achieve Excellence

People in Los Angeles often joke that "you are your car." Indeed, certain inferences are made about you based on the vehicle you drive. For example, driving a Mercedes or BMW might imply financial success while owning a SUV might suggest a large family or active lifestyle and buying a Chevy might signal a driver with "middle America" ideals. These perceptions may or may not be true, but an image is created by which these drivers are judged.

The same holds true in the workplace. Inferences about peoples' abilities are based on the image they project. People are judged not only by the words they choose to articulate a thought, but also by the tone and body language used during the delivery. Competence is inferred by the way we speak about what we know. It is important to be mindful of the images you project, not so as to live up to the images of others, but to ensure that any inferences made about you accurately reflect who you are. To do so, you must develop effective communication skills. This is not to suggest that form is more important than substance. However, you do not want your "form" to impede your ability to project competency.

Use Your Blinkers to Signal Intent

Nothing is more frustrating on the road than when the driver in the next lane decides to cut in front of you without using a signal. So too in communication, you want to use your blinkers. Your body language plays an important role in how people receive your message. To ensure your body always supports your message, consider the following tips.

Dress for success. Business casual has created distinct challenges in today's workplace. It is more difficult to define

what dressing for success looks like. To state the obvious, your look should always be neat, ironed and professional. Pay attention to the details: hair, nails, shoe shine, etc. The packaging is important.

Make eye contact. Look people directly in the eye when you are speaking. This serves three purposes. 1) It demonstrates confidence. You appear in control. 2) It engages people. Your eyes are like magnets; people cannot look away. They will feel acknowledged and drawn in to the conversation. 3) It provides instant feedback to determine how your message is being received. You will be able to see if people are confused, doubtful, bored, etc., and adjust your message accordingly.

Use your body to project confidence. Your stance should convey power and authority. Stand tall with your shoulders back and your feet firmly planted about hips-width apart. This will allow you to balance your weight and minimize distracting shifts from leg to leg as well as rocking backing and forth or swaying which makes you look nervous and uncomfortable.

The same principle applies when seated. Your feet should be flat on the ground and your forearms should be placed on the table. Sit on the front two thirds of the chair to ensure you are sitting straight. While this is not the most comfortable way to sit, it is the most commanding. When you are in the listener role, you can assume a more comfortable position.

Understand the power of your voice. Your voice is a very powerful, seldom thought about, tool. Notice effective speakers. There is a pace and a rhythm to their speech patterns. They project their voices, use pauses for dramatic effect and always manage to have a conversational tone to better connect with the audience. Speak slowly, enunciate clearly and smile when appropriate to let your enthusiasm and energy come through.

Remember to breathe. If your speech pattern is peppered with "ums," "uhs," "ers," "you knows" and "likes," it is probably because you are nervous and aren't breathing properly. At the end of each sentence, take a breath, focus your eyes and deliver the next sentence or thought. Power is never rushed.

Avoid the Potholes

Avoid common errors that delude your perceived competence. Do **NOT**:

- Pose statements as questions. Say, *"Come to my office at 3:00 p.m."* instead of *"Could you come to my office for a meeting at 3:00?"* Asking a question suggests the listener has an option. If you are in a supervisory position, you may not want to provide the option. It dilutes your perceived power.

- <u>Use disclaimers to introduce ideas</u>. Avoid beginning statements with *"This may not be right..."* or *"maybe I am missing something..."* It undermines your perceived confidence. Simply state the idea. If you are wrong, you will be told.

- <u>Tag questions onto statements.</u> Saying, *"That was a very productive meeting, wasn't it?"* makes you sound unsure. Your intent may have been to invite a response, but a better way to do that is to ask, *"What did you think of the meeting?"*

- <u>Introduce multiple subjects</u>. *"I think this draft is sloppy and unacceptable"* vs. *"This draft is sloppy and unacceptable."* It is safe to assume the listener understands if you are saying it, it is what you think. Your goal is to focus the listener on the true subject, the draft.

- <u>Use inappropriate words</u>. Some words don't belong in business. There is never a need for expletives, racial epithets or sexually charged language. Also be mindful of how you use words such as "like," "you know" and other colloquialisms. They signal a lack of polish and professionalism.

To ensure you deliver a powerful, listener-friendly message every time, deliver information in clusters of three. There is a rhythm to speaking that way that makes it easy for the listener to focus and retain information.

> *"Let's look at the **problem, cause** and **solution...**"*
> *"I will share the **facts,** our **analysis** and **recommendations...**"*
> *"There are **three important points** to consider..."*
> *"**Three factors** are driving this decision..."*
> *"**Three reasons** to move ahead are..."*

Remember, communication involves the intentions and actions of the speaker as well as the interpretations of the listener. While the person delivering the message knows exactly what is meant to be conveyed, the words chosen and the manner used to present the information may support or completely negate the intent. And sometimes, no matter how clearly the intended message was presented, listeners receive information through their own set of filters, which may distort the intended message and result in miscommunication.

Drive Defensively

You cannot control how other people share or process information. But you can consider their style and adapt your own style to improve communication. The purpose of adjusting your style to others is not simply to be nice. It is more self-serving than that. By giving your listeners what THEY need, you are more likely to get what YOU need from the exchange. For example, is your listener a fast-moving, action-oriented extrovert or a quiet, thoughtful introvert? Is this someone who likes lots of details and information or only bottom-line information? Is this someone with whom you can think out loud or someone who only wants to hear the end decision? Answers to these questions can help you adjust your presentation.

Learning to adapt to others is critical in every aspect of your professional life—from networking and interviewing, to supervising and delegating, to working with clients, peers and superiors. It is also a basic life skill that can be used to enhance your personal life. By being mindful of your own behavioral tendencies, you can improve your communication skills and, ultimately, your likeability.

Do not discount the importance of likeability in the workplace. When two people with equal competencies emerge for a promotion, a plum assignment or new position, the one people LIKE will always win. You don't need to buy everyone gifts to get them to like you. You simply need to learn how to express information clearly and succinctly and, most importantly, in the manner in which your listeners need to hear it. Whether delegating to a staff member, interacting with a client or interviewing with a potential employer, strong communicators have a distinct advantage in the world because they know how to relate to people.

At the end of the day, results are what counts. Deliver complete, high-quality work, on time, every time. Continuously learn the law and always strive to give 110% in your day-to-day responsibilities. Your goal is to be the one your organization wants to keep and other organizations want to steal away. Always think beyond the requested assignment to fully understand the bigger picture; communicate effectively to become recognized as a person who is reliable, trustworthy, and likeable and can make things happen.

Summary

Effective communication is the ability to give others what they need so that you get what you need. While competency is the baseline, excellence is the goal. True excellence, and your ability to communicate that excellence, is the ticket to career security.

CHAPTER FOUR

Keep Your Eyes on the Road

Identify and Utilize Available Resources

Anticipate Roadblocks, Speed Bumps, and Potholes

Up until now, the focus has been on you. What YOU want and need; what YOU can do. But, it isn't only about you. External realities play a role in shaping your life and helping you define your career objectives. Pay attention to economic forces and world events and make sure you understand the established structure of the work. You need a thorough knowledge of the various levels of responsibility within your chosen field, the experience and training required, the logical career paths. You need to know what standards are used to judge performance, which behaviors are valued and what the salary range is. If you are unprepared, these "have tos" can create speed bumps and potholes and needlessly impact other priorities in your life.

Today's business world is changing constantly. As a consequence, employers seek people who are up-to-date both in their field and in the world around them. You want to be "interview ready" at all times, even when you love your current job. You should always be in career-building mode and consistently working at:

1) investigating the world of work;
2) identifying people, organizations and industries doing the type of work you are interested in doing;
3) cataloging your skills and understanding how they can be used in those settings;
4) learning the cultural norms and buzz words used in different settings or alternative careers;

5) uncovering live job openings you might not otherwise know about;

6) being knowledgeable about compensation levels.

Keep Your Eyes on the Road

The internet makes it easy to conduct such on-going research. There is a wealth of information beyond simple job listings that can assist you in keeping abreast of marketplace trends and highlight the skills you need to acquire to ensure employability. There are databases containing information about industry trends, specific company profiles, relocation information, salary levels, etc. With over 40,000 employment-related sites in existence, you are sure to find the preliminary information you need. But it can be overwhelming. There are so many resources and so many different things you can do on the web, it's hard to know just where to begin.

Even if you are not actively looking for a job, consider conducting a lifelong "passive job search." Make it a point to regularly view job postings at both the larger sites like *monster.com, hotjobs.com* or *careerbuilders.com* and the niche sites aimed at the legal profession or industry in which you have an interest. This will enable you to keep tabs on market activities and remain in the "information loop." Also, don't forget to visit trade or professional associations as well as alumni sites. Sign up for industry news alerts through professional associations or papers like *Law.com*. Once a month or even once a quarter is all the time you need to invest in such activities.

On-line networking is a new phenomenon and, while the jury is still out on its effectiveness, it may be worth exploring. To take advantage of this tool, you must join one or more of the discussion groups hosted on sites of professional associations, university alumni groups or newsgroups. To find the appropriate site, check out:

- Gateway to Associations at the American Society of Association Executives (www.asanet.org)
- Directory of U.S. and International Associations at www.weddles.com
- College and university alumni groups' sites www.google.com/universities.html
- "Groups" on www.google.com for newsgroups

Each group has a unique culture and standards of participation; however, there is an etiquette to observe that applies to all. First, honestly provide the information requested by the group or moderator. While some groups allow anonymous participation, the best rule is to be open and honest about who you are and how you hope to benefit from the group. Next, before you jump into the discussion, "watch" the conversation silently for a while to get a feel for how the members of the group interact. Begin slowly. Introduce yourself, make a comment or two and gauge the group's response. You may learn you need to adjust the tone or style of your messages. Finally, you must participate regularly in the groups you join and be generous in sharing your knowledge, expertise and personal network.

Pick Up Passengers: Developing Your Network

As useful as the internet is, you cannot hide behind your computer screen. You need to talk to people. People are the single most valuable resource. They have more current, detailed and accurate information about what is happening in the world of work than any website, book or article ever can. It is extremely important to use these relationships to broaden your field of vision in order to make informed, smart decisions. You can learn about upcoming assignments and projects, pro bono opportunities, career paths you never considered, job openings, market rates, shifts in business practices and industry trends, etc. Don't think in terms of identifying a single mentor to rely on for guidance. Instead think of creating a support system or Board of Advisors to tap during periods of assessment and transition. Don't limit yourself to mentors who look like you or share your interests. A network of mentors will allow you to learn from different styles, develop a range of skills and consider various perspectives of an issue.

EXERCISE: Identify Your Board of Advisors

List 10-15 people you consider career/life advisors.

1. _____   2. _____

3. _____   4. _____

5. _____   6. _____

7. _____   8. _____

9. _____   10. _____

11. _____ 12. _____

13. _____ 14. _____

15. _____

Solid mentor relationships evolve naturally. The key is your willingness to work hard and make the relationships worthwhile for the mentors because of your enthusiasm and commitment. A mentor is not someone who solves all your problems; you should not burden anyone with such a responsibility. Think of mentors as resources to help you plan and execute your career goals and help you navigate difficult situations.

You should be concerned with the process of building and using networks as a permanent aspect of your career, not just as a technique you use when looking for a new job. Develop relationships *within* your organization. You rely on your skills and experience to impact *what* work gets done. But knowing *how* work gets done within an organization depends upon the network of relationships that exists. And, who you know isn't always as important as who knows you. Network internally to increase the chances of making an impression on decision-makers; learn about departments beyond your own and monitor the rumor mill, but don't contribute to it. Volunteer for committee assignments; attend events; eat lunch in the cafeteria. Be sure to establish a presence within your organization.

Understand office politics. It is not about "sucking up" or abandoning your own belief system to get ahead. Basically, it is the art of gaining "inside" access to the top people and positions in the organization. It is about making sure your contributions are valuable and visible and your goals are known to people in a position to help you achieve them. Use your own informed judgment to decide whom you respect most and let the opinions of those people matter most. You will always be affected by internal politics, so it is foolish to imagine yourself above it all and not get involved. Remember, those smart enough not to get involved in office politics are destined to be ruled by people of lesser intelligence.

Align your goals with the organization's goals and your boss' goals in order to expedite your career. Think about what keeps your boss up at night and attach yourself to the projects, people and areas that will able you to contribute in a way that makes the person's life easier. The trick is to create and understand your value to the boss and the organization while remaining true to yourself.

Develop, use and nurture personal relationships continuously. Keep in touch with people you meet throughout your career; don't wait until you "need" something from them. Establish a reputation for being helpful. Pass along useful information; introduce contacts to people in your network who might be helpful to them. Always look for ways to build bridges. Drop people notes occasionally or forward articles that may be of interest. People will remember your thoughtfulness and will be likely to return the favor.

Set a goal of establishing a set number of new acquaintances every month, both internally and externally. Join professional associations like the American Bar Association and local bar organizations, attend alumni events and participate in community activities to meet people and expand your professional network.

EXERCISE: Strengthen Your Network

List 5 actions you can take to strengthen your network <u>internally</u>.

1. _____

2. _____

3. _____

4. _____

5. _____

List 5 organizations you can join to strengthen your network <u>externally</u>.

1. _____

2. _____

3. _____

4. _____

5. _____

Get Out of Your Own Way

Anxiety often causes people to talk themselves out of participating in worthwhile activities that will increase their visibility. The fear of walking into a room filled with senior managers or total strangers is pervasive, cutting across boundaries of age, sex, race, socioeconomic level, professional and personal experience. But do whatever it takes to silence those discouraging voices in your head and motivate yourself to go anyway. Reassure yourself that once you are at the meeting or event, you will be fine. And, in the worst case scenario, if you <u>are</u> truly as miserable as those little voices in your head said you would be, you can always leave.

Challenge the myths you accepted as a child which may impede your ability to network effectively.

<u>Myth 1</u>: **It is impolite to talk about yourself.**
We have grown up believing that it is tacky to use people for personal gain. Being polite means being unobtrusive, not asking direct questions, not talking about our personal lives and drawing as little attention to ourselves as possible.

<u>Reality</u>: You have many things to *offer* as well as to gain. By freely acknowledging that attending an event is good for you because it will provide you with the opportunity to mingle with senior partners, or to develop business, or to meet potential employers or simply because it feels good to support a cause, you will eliminate the feeling of "dishonesty" and "tackiness" and be able to enjoy the event and participate fully. The networking opportunities will develop naturally.

<u>Myth 2</u>: **Don't talk to strangers.**
Ever since childhood parents instilled a fear about talking to people we did not know.

<u>Reality</u>: Consider the old saying, "Strangers are friends we haven't met yet." Think about what you have in common with others in the room. Are they all fellow attorneys or alumni or parents or church members or supporters of a political candidate, etc.? Determining the common bond makes it easier to approach people because they are no longer "strangers." You can then begin a conversation based on the common bond.

<u>Myth 3</u>: **Wait until you are properly introduced.**

<u>Reality</u>: Because it is not always feasible to be introduced by a mutual acquaintance, you may need to "properly introduce" yourself. Design a two- to three-sentence self-introduction that is clear, interesting and well-delivered. Your goal is to tell people who you are in a pleasant, positive manner. Naturally, what you say will depend on the nature of the event. For example:

- At a firm function: *"I recognize you from the elevator. I'm Katie McShane from the real estate group."*
- At an ABA convention: *"Hello, my name is Katie McShane. I am a real estate lawyer from NYC."*
- At a wedding: *"Hello. I don't believe we've met. I'm Katie McShane, former college roommate of the bride."*

Fear of rejection often stands in the way of approaching new people. This particular obstacle is more imagined than real. Very few people will be openly hostile or rude, if for no other reason than that it is bad manners. To help overcome this fear, try adapting a "host mentality." Hosts are concerned with the comfort of others and actively contribute to that comfort. By focusing on making others feel welcomed and included, you will become more comfortable. Find the person standing alone and introduce yourself. That person will likely be grateful. But, even if you **are** met with rudeness, do not take it personally. There may be a hundred reasons why that person is not receptive. Simply move on.

The best networkers put people at ease from the outset, and that makes conversations flow naturally. People who are most successful at it are those who genuinely like people. There is nothing calculated or manipulative about attending events to meet people. Remind yourself what has brought this particular group of people together and why it is important for you to be there.

Mastering the art of small talk will ease any prevailing networking anxieties and is simple to do. If you read a newspaper or watch CNN, you are ready for small talk. Use your observational skills to spark a lively, personal exchange. Consider one of the following three methods to get a conversation started.

1. Share an observation. Comment on a current, relevant news event or the situation at hand. Remark on the facility, food, organization, traffic, parking dilemma, etc. Remember, the comment ought to be positive and upbeat. Look for those bridges that have led the two of you to be in the same room.

2. Ask an open-ended question. (EXAMPLES: *"How long have you been a member of this organization?" "How do you fit into this picture?" "How do you know the bride or groom?"* Be careful not to fire off too many questions; you want to engage people in a conversation, not make them feel like they are being interrogated.

3. <u>Reveal something about yourself</u>. Disclosing something about you helps to establish vulnerability and approachability. (EXAMPLE: *"I have worked here for 3 months and have never been to the 48th floor."*) Volunteering information about you will make the other person feel safe about doing the same. Be careful not to reveal anything too personal that may burden the listener. (EXAMPLE: *"My spouse just asked me for a divorce."*)

Strong listening skills are critical tools to develop to become an effective networker. Be sure to:

- **Maintain eye contact** to appear interested.
- **Sit openly** to look involved and accessible.
- **Nod** to encourage speaker and show concern.
- **Probe** with open-ended questions *(What? Why? How?)* to ensure you LISTEN more than you talk and to show interest in what the speaker is saying.
- **Encourage** by saying things like *"I see"* or *"tell me more"* to collect better information/details.
- **Restate or paraphrase** what you have heard to verify understanding and avoid miscommunications.
- **Comment** to be an active participant in the conversation.

There is a natural rhythm to small talk. It should be interactive. After the initial introduction, the flow is probe, response, comment.

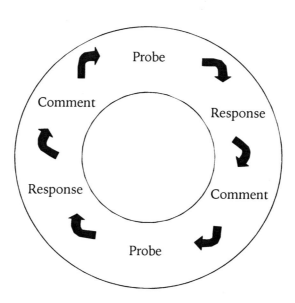

EXAMPLE:

Introduce: "I don't believe we've met. I'm Kate McShane."

Probe: "What department are you in?"

Response: *"I'm Jack DeMario, with the Banking group."*

Comment: "I'm in the tax group. That probably explains why we haven't run into each other."

Probe: "I understand your department has been unbelievably busy. Have you had any time to enjoy this great weather?"

Response: *"Yes. I managed to go waterskiing at Lake George last weekend."*

Comment: "Sounds like fun. I've never been waterskiing. Was that your first time?"

Even if the other person does not ask you any probing questions, you will be able to move the conversation forward. Naturally, the comment and follow-up probe should be based on what was said.

In any networking situation, it is wise to ask great questions and get others to do most of the talking. When it is your turn to talk, be mindful not to reveal proprietary information or spread gossip. Use good judgment. Imagine that everything you say is being piped into your boss's office.

The objective of attending an event is to meet a number of people, so it is important to circulate. Do not monopolize any one person's time, and do not allow your time to be monopolized by any one person. If someone has latched on to you, choose whether or not you want to make it your responsibility to take care of him/her throughout the event, thereby missing other opportunities present in the room. To make an exit, offer a connecting gesture like a handshake or a pat on the arm or shoulder and simply say:

- *"I am sure there are other people you need to talk to. I do not want to monopolize your time. It has been interesting speaking with you."*
- *"Excuse me, it was nice meeting you."*
- *"Excuse me; there is someone I need to say hello to."* (Make sure you move to another part of the room.)

To join the next group, simply say:

- *"Excuse me for interrupting, but I wanted to say hello."*

Another option would be to position yourself close to a group already engaged in conversation. Avoid groups that appear to be engaged in private, intimate conversations. Give facial feedback to comments. When you feel included (usually after you have established eye contact with someone in the group), feel free to join the conversation.

Remember to be open to others who may want to join a group you are already a part of. If you are doing the introductions, remember to "introduce up". Bluntly put, that means introduce the person with the lesser title to the person with the higher title (associate to the partner, partner to judge, etc.)

When attending events outside your office, business cards are a must in order to facilitate the exchange of information with people you meet. Place your business cards in an easy to reach place. You may want to invest in an attractive card carrying case. Once you have established rapport and decided you are interested in exchanging cards, offer yours first. People will typically return in kind. If there IS something you want from this person, decide whether it is appropriate to ask at that moment or if it would be sufficient to exchange cards and follow-up at a later date. Often times, the latter is the better option. Jot notes on the back of business cards to ensure you remember what was discussed. Keep in mind, the person who collects the most business cards is NOT the winner. If you are simply collecting cards, you probably haven't established an impression and it is likely the person will not remember you after the event.

Finally, you are completely responsible for what you bring into a room/ meeting and for what you project onto other people. Perception IS reality. Think about how other people see you. If you look and act like a loser, or someone who does not belong, that is exactly how people will respond to you. Your facial expression, posture and willingness to launch conversations matter. Dress and behave like a professional; be positive and upbeat; project a proud, confident image. Radiate confidence and people will be naturally drawn to you in every situation throughout your career. That will help to ensure that you have limitless resources in place when you need them.

Summary

Finding the right people to be part of your Board of Advisors takes work and initiative on your part. To avoid the career roadblocks:

- consciously deliver quality work with dignified behavior on a consistent basis;
- stay abreast of industry trends;
- grow contacts and relationships within your organization and industry.

Observe Posted Road Signs

Recognize the Signs of Change

Good drivers drive defensively. They are mindful of road and weather conditions; they are alert to road signs indicating a needed lane shift; and they plan alternative routes in case of emergency. Career strategists do the same. They pay attention to their environment in order to map out a path to avoid the obstacles while at the same time developing strategies to cope with the unexpected.

Transitions typically fall into one of four categories:

- **Anticipated and voluntary.** In a perfect world, all transitions would be the result of strategic decisions initiated by you.
- **Unanticipated and voluntary.** Sometimes, through no direct action on your part, the perfect opportunity lands in your lap. You have the luxury of accepting or declining the opportunity based on your current needs and interests.
- **Anticipated, but involuntary.** Many times people wait until others make a career decision for them. There may be warning signs that a transition is imminent, but rather than take action, you wait, allowing others to control your fate.
- **Unanticipated and involuntary.** Perhaps the most unsettling transitions fall into this category, typically because they tend to be negative. Everything was going along as usual—or so you thought. You believed you were productive; you know you've been busy. Your last reviews were positive and you even received a

year-end bonus. You didn't see any warning signs until the transition was thrust upon you.

To avoid experiencing involuntary transitions at work, pay close attention and constantly assess and reassess your current situation. Look for clues like:

- having difficulty with a supervisor
- being assigned less important tasks/duties
- not receiving bonus
- supervisors, colleagues, subordinates avoiding you
- receiving negative feedback/performance review
- not being personally productive or engaged in your job
- changes in the economy or business cycle that might impact your industry

If you see these signs, take action. Either fix the problem (if possible) or recognize you can't change the situation (and sometimes you can't through no fault of your own) and strategize your next move. Always try to avoid unanticipated and involuntary situations by actively anticipating and constructing self-directed voluntary transition plans.

EXERCISE: Is It Time to Change?

To determine if it is time to plan a career transition, place a check next to the statements that apply to you:

My job:

____ A   energizes rather than exhausts me

____ B   engrosses me to the extent that I lose track of time

____ C   involves skills that have always come naturally to me

____ D   is situated in a setting that I find comfortable (*do you prefer a large urban environment over a small town? a formal setting in an office building over a casual setting where the lawyers wear jeans to work?*)

____ E   capitalizes on my natural strengths, not my weaknesses

_____ F   involves the degree of human interaction that I find most comfortable *(do you want a job where you are on the phone for most of the day? in court? do you prefer a job where you primarily research cases in the law library?)*

_____ G   allows me to work with a supervisor I respect in a collegial environment

_____ H   is in a stable or growing industry/practice area

_____ I   provides opportunities to learn and grow professionally

_____ J   is something that I settled for rather than something I secretly hoped for

_____ K   is something that I feel I <u>should</u> do, or something I feel I <u>should</u> like

_____ L   forces me to act in a way that is highly unnatural to me *(for instance, your job calls for hours of library research and you are the type of person who hates to sit still)*

_____ M   fulfills my parents' or spouse's expectations, not my own

_____ N   bores me to the point of not caring about my work product

_____ O   makes me somewhat depressed at the thought of going to work each day

_____ P   is adversely affected by the current economic situation

_____ Q   performance has received negative feedback

_____ R   leaves me short-tempered at work and home

_____ S   is supervised by someone with an uneven temperament or questionable ethics

If you checked off three or more from A through I, you are on the right track. If you checked three or more from J through S, it is time to take action and map out a transition plan.

Brace Yourself for Change

One of the greatest impediments to change in any undertaking is that people withdraw from a situation rather than explore what the alternatives might be. It is possible to find joy in your work. Successful alternative arrangements in law practice **are** possible—-**if** you are willing to diverge from the norm. Trust yourself, others and the process to lead you to a better way. Once you have evidence of the possibilities, it will be easier to take action.

Understand that the way you think about a transition can make it easy to handle or impossible to manage. It is not the event that is determinative; rather, it is the way you choose to experience the event. Believe you have choices. Believe that you can create your own possibilities. Don't allow "shoulds" to force you down a path you do not want to go. Your only limitation is imposed by your imagination.

Your frame of mind affects your actions. For example:

BAD ATTITUDE	**IMPROVED ATTITUDE**
I screwed up. I'll never work again.	*It was a hard lesson to learn but I will be a better lawyer having learned it.*
There is no more bankruptcy work. I don't know how to do anything else.	*I will use what I know about bankruptcy to segue into debt financing work.*
The real estate market has dried up here. I will be living in my car soon.	*I'll relocate to ___ where the real estate market is hot.*

Attitude drives behavior and a positive attitude is critical to success.

This is especially true in the case of involuntary transitions. They are the most traumatic because they imply "failure." Even when you know it is time to leave your position, your ego takes a pounding when someone else tells you its time to move on. But consider the following failures:

- ☞ **Babe Ruth** struck out 1330 times en route to the Hall of Fame.
- ☞ **Elvis Presley** was banished from the Grand Ole Opry after only one performance and told, "You ain't going nowhere son."
- ☞ **Oprah Winfrey** was fired from her job as a TV reporter and advised, "You're not fit for TV."
- ☞ **Walt Disney**'s first cartoon production company went bankrupt.

☞ **John Grisham's** first novel, *A Time to Kill,* was rejected by 15 agents and a dozen publishing houses.

☞ **Edgar Allan Poe** was expelled from West Point.

☞ **Abraham Lincoln** lost eight elections, failed at two businesses and had a nervous breakdown before becoming our 16th President.

Nothing succeeds like failure. Learning opportunities, which are necessary for growth and development, sometimes come in the form of what would traditionally be defined as "failure." The world is filled with examples of people who used failure as a springboard to success. This is not to suggest you go out of your way to fail to achieve your career goals. Simply accept the fact that failures are going to happen. Readjust the prism through which you view such failures and you can use them to your advantage.

EXERCISE: How Do You Cope With Change?

Assess how effective you believe your coping strategies are in the following areas and rank yourself:

1 = Very Ineffective   2 = Ineffective   3= Average   4 = Effective   5 = Very Effective

_____	Taking action (creating plan and following through)
_____	Seeking advice
_____	Asserting yourself
_____	Generating possible alternatives/solutions
_____	Setting realistic goals
_____	Staying focused by being flexible
_____	Understanding transition process
_____	Rearranging priorities
_____	Redefining the transition in a positive light
_____	Engaging in humor
_____	Having faith
_____	Using positive self-talk
_____	Imaging desired outcome
_____	Maintaining focus
_____	Balancing work/family/leisure
_____	Playing
_____	Avoiding negativity (your own and that of others)
_____	Expressing emotion

_____	Engaging in physical activity
_____	Participating in counseling/support groups
_____	Managing your time
_____	Using a range of strategies
_____	Being patient
_____	**TOTAL**

If you have a LOW score (under 50), you may need to develop your skills in some of these areas to help ease any transition. A score between 50 and 90 suggests your coping skills are MODERATE. Look at how many skills you ranked 5. You may find you are using the same few strategies over and over again. Incorporate two or three additional strategies into your transition plan to enhance your coping abilities. Even a modest adjustment to your typical routine can have a significant ripple effect. A score above 90 indicates that you are well equipped to manage transitions.

Take Action

As you work on accepting change more readily, remember the important thing is that you take charge of your own career development. Identify the changes you need/want to make and then be proactive about making those changes happen. ASSUME RESPONSIBILITY. No one cares about your career development more than you do. Don't wait for others to lead you through the quagmire. Remember, planning your career is like solving a business problem. Define objectives, develop strategies, monitor progress and take corrective action when needed. The beauty of the career planning process is that YOU get to define the objectives based on your personal definition of success. Whatever option you choose, know that as long as you are able to demonstrate to employers that there is a well-thought-out, coherent plan aimed at building a portfolio of skills, the choice will be well received. It is scary to head into the unknown. But remember that basic principle you learned in high school physics: _Bodies in motion stay in motion; bodies at rest stay at rest._ Take action.

Think about the direction you'd like your life to take. Determine what type of experience you need in order to progress along your chosen career path. Stretch yourself to acquire new skills/knowledge to remain in constant demand and at the same time invest in developing an expertise. Such a strategy will enable you to have a competitive advantage. Specializing in one area alone can be risky, as real estate attorneys discovered in the 1980s. Market pressures may render you obsolete. But make sure you are not so much of a generalist that you have not developed proficiency in any particular skill. A balance of the two is a better strategy. Base your mix of expertise and flexibility on the overall development goal you set. Areas of new exposure are not limited to the development of technical expertise but include other more general skills as well. As you develop your technical skills, don't forget to focus on "soft" skills—things like working in teams, time management, negotiating, communicating, understanding diversity, delegating and adapting to change. Such intangibles are often "silent discriminators," indicating who is on the fast track and who is not. Soft skills enable you to apply your hard skills in a variety of situations, thereby increasing your value to the employer. By serving as an officer or director of community groups, on alumni boards, or in church and synagogue groups, you can build these skills. Experience gained in any situation counts.

You may determine that you are on the correct path. In that instance, your action plan would simply be to continue doing what you have been doing and reevaluate your progress annually to compare your achievements to your intended objectives. Each year, ask yourself:

- Am I satisfied with my current career/life situation?
- Has any new exposure sought been gained?
- Has my level of responsibility increased? Is that what I want?
- Does the current work environment continue to be receptive to my career objectives?
- Do I need to make any course corrections?

If the answer to these questions is no, you may determine that a change in employment, a redirection of your career path or an industry shift is in order. Do something to realign your career with your goals. Refer back to Chapter Two to review your 5-Year and Annual Plans.

Reality Check: Can You *Afford* to Change?

As you travel towards your dream, you want to position yourself to always be in the proper mental and financial state to take advantage of opportunities as they arise. Any change at work will impact your life, AND any change in your life may very well impact your work too. For example, embarking on a new job/career when you are in the middle of an unsettling divorce, tending to a terminally ill family member or starting a family may not be a good idea. Do what you can to manage such events to limit their impact on your career choices, but accept that some things are simply beyond your control.

While you can't always control your emotional state, you can typically control your financial situation. Tend to your finances early in your career. Managing your finances from the beginning of your career will provide you with the freedom to pursue opportunities of interest throughout your career. Financial security creates an air of confidence and independence and allows you to follow your passions and live well.

How much money do you need to earn in order to maintain your current lifestyle? Just because a $45,000-a-year legal services job may be out of the question does not mean that a $150,000-a-year large firm position is the only alternative. There are a substantial number of legal, legal-related and non-legal positions that pay very acceptable salaries. Write out a detailed budget for yourself and your family. This preliminary investigation into salary will help you later on as you contemplate opportunities. Use the following worksheet to chart your annual living expenses.

Monthly Cash Outflow

Mortgage/Rent _____

Investment Tax (interest **x** tax bracket) _____

Savings _____

Groceries _____

Gas & Electric _____

Telephone _____

Cable/Internet _____

Loans

    Student _____

    Car _____

    Personal/Home Equity _____

Car Expenses (gas, parking, maintenance) _____

Public Transportation/Tolls _____

Professional Membership Fees _____

Charitable Contributions _____

Child Care _____

Tuition _____

Pets/Pet Care   _____

Insurance

    Health   _____

    Homeowners   _____

    Disability   _____

    Life   _____

Medical/Dental   _____

Health Club Fees   _____

Clothes   _____

    Laundry/Dry Cleaning   _____

Entertainment

    Eating Out   _____

    Vacation   _____

    Magazines/Newspapers/Books   _____

    Movies/Theater   _____

    Computer Software   _____

    Hobbies   _____

Home Expenses   _____

Gifts   _____

Personal Care (haircuts, etc)   _____

TOTAL MONTHLY OUTFLOW   _____

x 12 = Annual Living Expenses   _____

It is important to recognize that what you **need** is not necessarily what employers will think you are **worth.** While the seller may set the price, it is ultimately the buyer who determines the value. (We will talk more about this in Chapter Ten).

Do not hesitate to spend some of your own money to ensure your employability. Invest in training, career development and education. Pay for your own CLEs if your employer won't cover the expense. Enroll in "non-legal" seminars and workshops covering topics like public speaking, management or client development to enhance your portfolio of skills. Consider periodically consulting with a career counselor to keep you focused and on track.

Make wise choices about which investments to make. Education and training alone don't ensure success, as many well-educated, unemployed professionals can tell you. For example, while an advanced degree **may** increase your marketability in some of the more technical fields such as tax law or academia or help you transition from one specialty to another by providing intense training and knowledge quickly, an advanced degree could also **decrease** your marketability. Some major legal employers have their own training programs and hesitate to hire candidates with advanced degrees who command higher salaries. Employers also sometimes view LL.M. degrees as a way to whitewash a less than stellar J.D. performance. Before you decide to invest in any educational program, make sure you are doing it because you have a genuine interest in the subject matter not simply to add a credential to your resume. Find out if your employer (or target employer) values the extra schooling and do a cost/benefit analysis. Remember not only to factor in tuition and related school costs but also your lost wages during the time you are in graduate school.

Whether you are in a transition voluntarily or involuntarily, you will no doubt ask yourself questions like:

- Is there some way to combine my practice with my other, equally important interests?
- Are there jobs available at my level and salary expectations or will I have to settle for less?
- Do I give up the practice of law altogether and if so, what else can I do?

These questions can be overwhelming because there are no immediate answers. Don't get stymied and opt to stay stuck in an unhappy situation or simply avoid the questions altogether. Playing it safe and staying in a position you have outgrown will damage your career. Most people end up happier after a transition. The hard part is living through the unavoidable discomfort and uncertainties.

Summary

How often you change positions, jobs or careers typically matters less than WHY. However, you must be able to articulate a logical progression down a coherent path. Do you have a good story line? Employers easily understand people moving on to develop new skills or industry knowledges or to broaden their portfolio of experiences. However, when the moves appear to be a chase for salary increases or fancy titles only, your loyalty and perhaps judgment may be questioned. The onus is on you to articulate the story line and illustrate the wisdom in the decisions you have made along the way. Refer back to the *Reflections* exercise completed in Chapter One to help you create your story line. It is necessary to be:

- **Proactive.** Career development is a process that requires initiative.
- **Self-aware.** You must understand—and be able to articulate—the value you add based on your abilities and attitudes.
- **Dedicated to continuous learning.** You must regularly benchmark your skills and create a personal and professional development plan to keep your skills current.
- **Future-focused.** Constantly look ahead to assess customer needs and business trends. Consider the impact of those trends on your work and your development plan.
- **Flexible.** Anticipate change and be ready to adapt quickly.

It cannot be said enough—**you have the power to create the career—and life—you want,** but you have to DO something to make it happen.

CHAPTER SIX

Standing at the Crossroad

How to Launch a Job Search

At some point you are likely to encounter a roadblock that indicates a job change is in order. If you have heeded the advice in this book so far and have continually dedicated a percentage of your busy schedule to catalogue your skills, to stay abreast of trends and themes and to strengthen your network, you are well positioned to conduct a job search. If not, you have some preliminary steps to take before heading into the marketplace. But not to worry: It is never too late to start.

EXERCISE: Are You Ready to Roll?

To determine if you are ready to launch your job search, answer the following questions.

Yes   No

_____   _____   Can I articulate my skills and special knowledge—as well as the "value added" I can contribute? (If no, return to Chapter Two)

_____   _____   Do I know what I need to feel happy and successful? (If no, return to Chapter Two)

_____   _____   Am I aware of the major trends in the field/industry and the implications of these   changes for my career? (If no, review Chapter Four)

_____   _____   Have I/Am I ready to develop a network of people to assist me in my efforts? (If no, return to Chapter Four)

Understand the Job Search Process

Most lawyers think of the job search as a linear process; respond to ads by drafting resumes & cover letters, interview for positions and then consider offers. However, the process is more complex than that. Consider the following chart.

JOB SEARCH PROCESS

Step 1
SELF ASSESSMENT
- evaluate motivations
- identify values, skills & abilities
- recognize preferred work styles
- set goals
- examine interests
- consider temperament
- list accomplishments
- recognize special knowledge
- evaluate experiences
- acknowledge educational level

Step 2
MARKET RESEARCH
- pay attention to opportunities
- join professional organizations
- read trade papers
- talk to business associates, friends and family members
- surf the web
- research individuals, organizations and communities

NEW CAREER/JOB

Step 4
IMPLEMENTATION
Conduct:
- research
- informational interviews
- job interviews
- salary negotiations

Step 3
SKILL DEVELOPMENT
Learn how to:
- conduct research
- develop contact lists
- interview for information
- interview for jobs
- draft resumes and cover letters
- negotiate salary
- assess offers

The job search process is actually circular and continuous. Once you have completed steps one and two, you need to step up your efforts and transform that self-knowledge and market knowledge into the job of your dreams. But how? DRIVE!!

D ream
R eview your goals
I dentify the options
V erbalize your special talents
E xecute

Dream

Ask yourself: What is my dream job? Don't worry, *for the moment,* if the job makes sense or if you are overqualified, underqualified, too young, too old, etc. Don't worry about pay scales or additional training needed. For the moment, just think about what you would like to **do**. Once you identify the dream, the practicalities will come into play to shape the direction of your job search. The trick is to not let those practicalities stifle the dream prematurely. There may be ancillary careers that can put you in the arena of your dream job.

For example, let's suppose the dream job is to be a pitcher for the New York Yankees. Rather than simply dismiss that as an impractical dream, brainstorm what other positions might be available that incorporate a passion for baseball with your current skill sets. Are there legal or management positions at organizations such as Major League Baseball, Tops Baseball Cards, Spalding, Nike, the players' union, etc.? What firms represent the owners, players or specific teams? Have any of the players established youth baseball camps, restaurants or clothing lines? What role could a lawyer play in those ventures? Think creatively. Think big. Once you have a general direction, it will be easier to strategize how to get there.

The good news is that the options both inside and outside of traditional law practice are unlimited. The bad news is the alternatives both inside and outside of traditional law practice are unlimited. That reality paralyzes some people. With unlimited options, how do you know where to even begin?

Start by believing you have choices. The job market, which is conservative and myopic by nature, wants you to keep doing what you have been doing. You are most understandable to potential employers in terms of your past career choices and your tenure in prior settings. Understandably, your most recent position is the clearest indication of your highest level of competency. The mere fact of change can raise questions about your motives. Are you running toward something or away from something? It is important to stay in control of your search to ensure that these market forces do not dictate your choices. That is why self-assessment is so important. It enables you to believe you have options, create your own opportunities and articulate the progression of your career path in a coherent manner.

Review Your Goals

Review the Goal Sheets you completed in Chapter Two. Will a move take you closer to fulfilling the long-term goals you have established? Also, consider how a move will impact the rest of your life. You are more than just a practicing attorney. You may also be a spouse, a parent, a friend, a child, a PTA volunteer, a civic leader, etc. Will a change allow you to project the image you want while at the same time allowing you to be true to your own personal identity? Does it fit in with your overall plan or, in the alternative, are you prepared to revamp the plan? Either option is acceptable so long as it is a conscious choice. These questions are not meant to stymie you; they are meant to force you to check your ego and make sure any change is made for the proper reasons.

Identify the Options

For most lawyers, an adjustment of practice area, setting, size of firm or location or shift to flex-time is all they need to find the "dream job" and achieve life/work balance. For others a move in-house, to a bar association or education institution is sufficient. Still others parlay industry knowledge developed as a lawyer to pursue non-traditional opportunities. You are limited only by your personal preferences, imagination and willingness to devote the time and energy necessary to explore the possibilities.

EXERCISE: Identify Your Options

STEP ONE: Consider the various *setting* options. Circle the ones that hold the greatest appeal.

LAW FIRMS	*Representing*
Solo practice	Business
2-10	Business with pro bono opportunities
11-25	Businesses and individuals
26-50	Individuals (defense or plaintiff)
51-100	Individuals (non-litigation)
101-250	Public Interest
251-500	Other
500 plus	

PRACTICE AREAS

Administrative Law

Admiralty & Maritime Law

Adoption

Agriculture Law

Alternative Dispute Resolution

Antitrust & Trade Regulation

Asbestos Mesothelioma

Aviation

Banking & Finance Law

Bankruptcy Law

Business & Commercial Law

Business Organizations

Child Support

Civil Rights

Communications & Media Law

Constitutional Law

Construction Law

Consumer Protection

Contracts

Criminal Law

Criminal Law—Federal

Custody & Visitation

Debtor Creditor

Discrimination

Divorce

DUI DWI

Education Law

Elder Law

Election Campaign & Political Law

Eminent Domain

Employment Law—Employee

Employment Law—Employer

Energy Law

Entertainment, Sports & Leisure
 Law

Environmental Law

Estate Planning

Ethics & Professional Responsibility

Family Law

Franchising

Gaming Law

Government Agencies & Programs

Government Contracts

Health & Health Care Law

Immigration & Naturalization Law

Insurance Law

Intellectual Property Law

International Law

Internet—Cyberspace

Labor Law

Land Use & Zoning

Landlord Tenant

Legal Malpractice

Lemon Law

Litigation & Appeals

Mediation & Collaborative Law

Medical Malpractice

Military Law

Motor Vehicle Accidents — Plaintiff

Native Peoples Law

Natural Resources Law

Nursing Home

Patents

Personal Injury—Defense

Personal Injury—Plaintiff

Probate & Estate Administration

Products Liability Law

Professional Malpractice Law

Real Estate Law

Science & Technology Law

Securities Law

Sexual Harassment

Social Security—Disability

State, Local & Municipal Law

Taxation Law

Toxic Torts

Trademarks

Traffic Violations

Transportation Law

Trusts

Wills

Workers' Compensation Law

IN-HOUSE COUNSEL

Businesses, Non-Profits, Hospital/Health Organizations, Banking/ Financial Services, Real Estate Development, Insurance, Accounting, Management Consulting, Foundations, Labor Unions, Trade Associations, Colleges & Universities, Museums, Professional Societies, Religious Organizations

GOVERNMENT

Federal (Executive, Legislative, Judicial-trial, Judicial-appellate, U.S. Attorney, Armed Forces)

State (Executive, Legislative, Judicial-trial, Judicial-appellate, Attorney General)

County/Regional (Executive, Legislative, Judicial-trial, Judicial-appellate, District Attorney)

Municipal (Executive, Legislative, Judicial-trial, Judicial-appellate, City Solicitor)

PUBLIC INTEREST

Legal Services, Law Centers, Policy & Research, Public Defenders, Social Action Organizations, Non-Profit Organizations, Clinics

ACADEMIA

Faculty, Administration, Library, Clinics

STEP TWO: Review the list of job titles below and circle the ones that sound interesting. Keep in mind, this list is by no means exhaustive.

ACADEMIA

Dean
Assistant Dean
  Career Planning
  Student Services
  Alumni Relations
  Registrar
  Financial Aid
Law Professor
Clinical Education Director
Researcher
Librarian

BANKING

Trust Officer
Commercial Loan Administrator
Estate Administrator
Credit Analyst
Compliance Director
Relationship Manager
Portfolio Manger

BUSINESS

General Counsel
Human Resources Director
Labor Union Manager
Labor Negotiator
Sales
Affirmative Action Director
Business Valuations Expert
Pension /profit sharing planner
Ombudsman
Arbitrator
Corporate Secretary
Ethical Advisor
CEO
CFO
CIO
Risk Manager
Compliance Director
Controller
Forensic Accountant
Corporate Strategists

COMMUNICATION
Legal publication editor/writer
Legal reporter
Legal research services
Writer/Novelist
Marketing
Communications Director
Publisher
Publicist
Screenwriter

CONSULTING SERVICES
CLE Instructor/Director
Legal Placement Consultant
Paralegal Placement
Legal Secretary Placement
Temporary Attorney Placement
Jury Consultant
Deposition Training/Videotaping
Expert Witness Consultant
Trial Preparation Services
Court Reporting
Investigator
Document Production Services
Technology Support
Litigation Support
Legal Database Developers

FINANCIAL SERVICES
Stockbroker
Hedge Fund Manger
Derviatives Expert
Investment Banker
Financial Planner
Analyst
Tax Manager

GOVERNMENT
Agency Staff Attorney
Judge Advocate
Judge
Magistrate
Legislative Analyst

Lobbyist
CIA/FBI Agent
City/County Clerk
Court Administrator
Court Reporter
Foreign Service Officer
Mediator/Arbitrator
Civil/Criminal Investigator

INSURANCE
Defense
Sales
Claims Adjuster

MANAGEMENT
Law Firm Administrator
Executive Director
Finance
Technology Services
Librarian
Recruiting
Professional Development
Marketing
Diversity

POLITICS
Elected Official
Campaign Manager
Fundraiser

PUBLIC SERVICE
Legal Clinic Managing Attorney
Executive Director
Volunteer Legal Services Director
Lawyer Referral Service Director
Development Director

REAL ESTATE
Developer
Land Use Developer
Commercial/Residential Sales
Property Manger
Asset Manager

Verbalize Your Special Talents

Use the information uncovered in Chapter Two to create a marketing statement that clearly and precisely describes your skills and talents as well as the type of position you are seeking.

EXERCISE: Draft Your Marketing Statement

I am seeking a position as a _____ *in house counsel*

in a setting such as _____ *Corporation*
(organization type)

in _____ *NY metro area*
(geography)

utilizing my special knowledge in the areas of

Litigation , *Employment* ,

Compliance , & *Strategic thinking* .

My skills in *Writing* , *Analysis* ,

& ~~problem solving~~ ~~management strategy~~ should be helpful in achieving my goal(s)

of ~~finding~~ *specializing my broad, diverse*
experience in a more focused in
house practice.

Once you have the basic information assembled, massage the sentence structure and syntax until you create a self-introduction that rolls easily off your tongue.

Execute

A job hunt does not have to be a devastating experience; it does not take guts so much as it requires thought, persistence and a willingness to sacrifice monetary pleasures for a long-term goal. Keep in mind that job searches take a long time. Legal search consultants suggest that people should expect to be in the process one month for every $10, 000 they earn. A creative job search may take longer. Remember, it is not necessarily the most qualified person who gets the job; rather, it is the person most skilled at finding a job. Focus on the *PROCESS*.

Step 1: <u>ALLOCATE A SPECIFIC AMOUNT OF TIME</u>

To get yourself started, you must decide how much time you can realistically devote to your search. If you are currently working, consider 2-3 hours per week; if you are unemployed, consider 5-7 hours a day. Maintaining a **steady and consistent** effort throughout your search will be one of the most important elements in determining your success. A "start and stop" approach almost always leads you back to square one at each juncture. Working in bursts of activity will ensure failure. Sending out a stack of resumes 6 months ago does not entitle you to say "I've been looking for 6 months" if you have done nothing to follow up.

Step 2: <u>ADHERE TO A SCHEDULE</u>

Regardless of how many hours you have allocated to the process, work out a schedule and make a personal commitment to stick to it. During those reserved hours, your job search must be your primary focus. This is the time committed to self-assessment exercises, making phone calls, conducting research, etc. Do not allow yourself to be interrupted by running errands, baby sitting, etc. By adhering to a schedule, you will reduce the insecurity most job seekers feel because you will be in control. You will also be able to chart your progress.

Step 3: <u>SELECT A SYSTEM TO RECORD YOUR ACTIVITIES</u>

Whether you opt for a notebook and pen or an elaborate computer-based system, you must develop a system for recording your activities in order to easily retrieve important data and to ensure appropriate follow-up actions. You may want to visit an office products or discount store to give you some ideas about what kind of system will work best for you. (See sample Activity Sheet on next page.)

Step 4: <u>USE ALL AVAILABLE RESOURCES</u>

Many lawyers are unaware that they can schedule individual appointments with a counselor at their law school's Office of Career Services. An initial appointment with a career counselor (generally free of charge) can provide information about the type of services your school offers its alumni. For example, nearly every law school has created a newsletter or intranet job board containing job listings of lateral positions. These offer a wealth of information and possible job leads because many schools receive from their alumni listings that are not published elsewhere. A number of law schools also trade their listings with other schools, thus enabling their graduates

SAMPLE ACTIVITY SHEET

Target Employer (name, address, phone, email)	Primary Contact	Date Contacted (6-10 days after initial contact)	Follow-up action	End Results (i.e., source of lead)	Additional Info

access to job listings from schools located in different geographic areas. Every law school's Office of Career Services contains a mini library for graduates to research job opportunities, jot down listings, and read directories, books and periodicals relevant to the job search. By utilizing your career library, you can save a lot of expensive subscription costs and have access to a multitude of resources.

State and local bar associations have done a commendable job supplementing the work of the law schools in offering support groups, workshops and seminars for their membership. Many offer seminars featuring career experts, and job listings to its members. Finally, don't forget to use people in your own network of friends and colleagues, as well as your Board of Advisors, to ask for advice, information and referrals.

Your emotional well-being deserves attention and care throughout the process. In fact, your productivity and ultimate success depend on it. This is the hardest part for lawyers. Being associated with a particular firm or organization can be such an important part of a person's life and identity. The thought of a transition—even a voluntary one—creates a tremendous sense of anxiety. The things people typically fear most about a job change include:

- disruption of familiar and comfortable routines
- possibility of unanticipated events that may result from change
- risking current job security
- financial considerations
- self-doubts
- losing status/identity
- not getting along with new co-workers/supervisors

Analyze the panic. How real are these fears? How can you prepare for, minimize or render any of these scenarios temporary? Share your anxieties with friends/family. Not only can these people be great sounding boards but they can also help you spot flaws in your approach. However, if you believe a well-meaning spouse or parents will drive you crazy by trying to be helpful or asking too many questions or by just plain nagging, politely ask them to leave you alone while you sort through things. Consider reaching out to a member of your Board of Advisors or retaining a career counselor for any needed assistance.

Keep in mind a change in your life naturally means a change in the life of your family members. They may be scared or have questions too. Do not try to protect loved ones by acting in control. They will be more supportive if they know what is going on and understand how they can be helpful.

Because the very nature of the job search process invites rejection, it is important to design strategies to work through the rejection so that you have the energy to move on to the next call or meeting or interview, which may be the one where you land the perfect job. Allow yourself time to be with the important people in your life who can provide support, encouragement and perhaps a few laughs during this challenging time. Do not feel guilty about enjoying something or goofing off periodically. Exercise, take a short trip, tackle a project or read a novel. A short time away from your job search may allow you to return with renewed vigor and energy.

Finally, in order to maintain a sustained, consistent effort, break the job search process down into small, manageable steps. If you wake up each morning and declare, "Today I will find a new job," you are setting yourself up for failure; you will become overwhelmed and subsequently paralyzed. Use the following Weekly Action Sheet to establish short-term goals and monitor your progress.

Summary

Because you have heeded the advice of the first five chapters of **Navigating Detours on the Road to Success**, you are well positioned to conduct a job search. Without even realizing it, you have incorporated Steps 1 & 2 of the Job Search Process into your work routine. The following chapters will demonstrate how to "give it the gas" and get to your destination more quickly.

WEEKLY ACTION PLAN WORKSHEET
Week of _____

1) This week my **goal** is to commit _____ hours to my job search.

2) I will **accomplish** the following tasks:

   a) _____

   b) _____

   c) _____

3) The things I must **do** to accomplish these tasks are: Complete

   a) _____ [   ]

   b) _____ [   ]

   c) _____ [   ]

4) Possible **obstacles** and **challenges** to prevent me from accomplishing tasks:

   _____

   _____

   _____

5) Strategies to **overcome** obstacles and challenges:

   _____

   _____

   _____

CHAPTER SEVEN

CareerTravel Aids

How to Use the Internet, Recruiters and Contacts

Looking for a new job will be a less daunting task for those who have invested the time to stay abreast of trends and opportunities in the profession in an on-going, consistent manner. (And for those who have not, it is not too late to get in the game.) It is now a matter of increasing those efforts to secure a new position. There are many tools at your disposal including newspapers and periodicals, professional recruiters, personal contacts and the internet. When used correctly and in combination with each other, these resources can help you to be proactive, informed and selective in your job search and ultimately, to control your destiny.

In Chapter Four, we discussed how to use the internet to conduct a "passive job search." By reviewing relevant employment sites, you have developed an understanding of how your skills and talents can be used in the world of work. Now that you are in an active job search, it is time to "give it the gas" and take your research efforts to the next level.

Use the Internet

The internet is a powerful tool, chock full of useful information. For an active job search, view job postings at both the larger sites like *monster.com, hotjobs.com* or *careerbuilders.com* and the niche sites aimed at the legal profession or industry you are targeting at least once a week. View trade or professional associations as well as alumni sites.

Identify 10-12 sites that are most likely to serve you best (see Appendix). To help you assess which are the best ones to use, consider:

• the number and kinds of jobs posted on the site;

- the primary salary levels of the posted jobs;
- the cost of using the site;
- the availability of other job search information, such as interview preparation, negotiating tips, etc.

You also want to make sure the site is well maintained, regularly updated and easy to navigate.

EXERCISE: Identify 10–12 Relevant Websites

1. _____

2. _____

3. _____

4. _____

5. _____

6. _____

7. _____

8. _____

9. _____

10. _____

Consider using electronic "job agents." This is a function offered by some websites that allows you to enter your employment objectives and be automatically notified whenever there is a match. As powerful and convenient as they are, job agents should not be a substitute for the host of other activities involved in an effective job search; they are just one of many resources available to you.

Finally, if you choose to post your resume in a searchable database, make sure there is a confidentiality feature so that your contact information will not be distributed until you agree to release it to a specific employer. Also, make sure those resumes are dated so you can confirm a resume is the most current version.

If you see a job in which you have an interest, follow the application instructions. But don't stop there. Review the members of the Board of Advisors you identified in Chapter Four. Is it possible that someone on that list knows someone who works at the organization to which you have applied? Is there someone else in your network that may be able to help? Do not assume that because you discussed your career goals with them earlier they will automatically think of you. Use this as an opportunity to reconnect with your contact and remind them you are actively looking. Contact that person and say something like:

"John, I wanted to let you know that I applied for a position at XYZ corporation advertised on hotjobs. I remembered that they were a client of yours. Could I ask you to mention my name to your contact?"

Or

"Do you know anyone in the legal department that I could follow up with?"

Let's assume you do not know anyone with a connection to the employer. Call the organization's general number and ask for the proper spelling of the head of human resources department or the general counsel. Do not ask to *speak* with that person. It will be obvious that it is a solicitation of some sort. Make two phone calls. That way, when you call back later in the day and ask for Mary Jones, your call will be less suspect and you will have a greater chance of getting through. Follow up directly with that person to ensure that your resume has been received and ask if there is any additional information you can supply. Always take the *"how can I be helpful to you"* approach rather than the *"why haven't you called me in for an interview yet?"* approach.

Remember, there is an abundance of information beyond simple job listings that can assist you in your search. Use Hoovers On-line at *hoovers.com* to acquire the basics on a company's industry, products or services, size, executive team, locations and contact information. Use *Google.com* or *askjeeves.com* to research comparable organizations in which you might have an interest and check the home pages of those target employers to view job listings. Finally don't forget to show such lists to your contacts and ask if they can introduce you to someone at these organizations or if they can think of other organizations that you should add to your list.

Because you need to be prepared to have the salary conversation whenever the employer brings it up, prepare by reviewing annual salary surveys published by trade magazines and associations to get a ballpark figure of the going rates. Keep in mind that these numbers are not absolute figures; they should be used to help you calculate an appropriate salary range for positions based on a realistic assessment of what the market will command. This information will be critical during the negotiating phase of a job search campaign. Look for:

- *AmLaw 100,* which examines gross revenues, profits, and compensation levels for America's highest-grossing firms. Periodically, *The American Lawyer* also publishes mid-level associate salary surveys.
- The National Association for Law Placement's annual *Associate Salary Survey* summarizes national salary information for each associate year. The information is grouped by firm/office size, region and population of the metropolitan area. NALP also publishes *Public Interest and Government Salaries,* which provides information by years of experience. Visit www.NALP.org.
- Altman Weil Pensa annually publishes a *Survey of Law Firm Economics,* as well as a *Small Law Firm Economic Survey,* and *Law Department Compensation Benchmarking Survey.*
- Abbott, Langer & Associates' *Compensation of Legal and Re-lated Jobs (Non-Law Firm)* provides information on in-house counsel positions sorted by geographic location, type of employer, size of organization and field of specialization. They also publish *Compensation in Nonprofit Organizations.*
- *The American Almanac of Jobs and Salaries* provides salary information for a range of careers annually.
- *The Office of Personnel Management* provides information on government salaries at http://www.opm.gov/oca/05tables/index.asp

Also check out www.payscale.com; www.vault.com; www.salary.com and www.law360.com.

Finally, you must understand what you can expect from the internet. Sitting home in your pajamas applying to jobs on-line is not likely to yield the results you want. Studies indicate that approximately 4-6% of new hires come from job boards. The percentage is higher for company websites, but it is still under 25%. If you dedicate 90% of your time to an effort with such a low rate of return, you will be missing opportunities. While the internet is a great tool, you must use it in conjunction with every other resource available to you in order to be effective.

Read Newspapers and Periodicals

Don't neglect the "old fashioned" method of reviewing the classified sections of local legal and non-legal publications. You may uncover positions there and then use the internet to find out more in-depth information. Again, don't forget to loop back to your contacts to see if anyone you know has a connection to the employer.

Talk to Recruiters

Candidates who come through a recruiter come with a huge price tag, usually about a third of the candidate's first-year salary. By using your contacts to stay in the information loop and uncovering openings, you can approach employers directly, thereby eliminating the fee and making yourself a more attractive candidate. However, with that said, it is still important for job seekers to learn how to incorporate headhunters into their job search activities.

Because it is the headhunters' business to know what is happening in the marketplace, they can provide valuable information about things like which academic and professional credentials are hot and which geographic regions have increasing legal opportunities. If a recruiter calls you, take the call. Keep an open mind at least long enough to hear the pitch and see what you can learn.

Refer to the annual pull-out sections of the **American Lawyer** or the **Legal Times** for names of executive recruiters. Listed by geographic location, these publications provide information about the company's size, number of attorney placements made and other important information. You may also want to visit the **National Association of Legal Search Consultants** website (www.NALSC.org), which provides direct links to local search firms.

Before you decide to proceed with a headhunter, ask what procedures will be followed as well as what precautions will be taken to ensure your privacy and maintain the confidentiality of all transactions. Generally, the process follows a similar pattern. First, you will be interviewed by the headhunter to determine what you are looking for and if any suitable positions currently exist. If so, you will be asked for your permission to send the resume to the employer. Do not give blanket approval to distribute your resume everywhere, particularly if you are working with several recruiters. That could create a fee dispute and cause problems for the employer. If you learn of an opening independently, do not let the headhunter send your resume. Send it yourself to avoid the price tag.

The headhunter's task is to present your credentials in such a way as to entice the employer to want to meet you. Provide the headhunter with as much relevant information as possible to make that step easy. Once that is accomplished, you can expect multiple interviews with the employer. If the employer determines that you are the candidate he wants to hire, you will begin salary negotiations through the headhunter.

It is important to remember that the fee-paying employer is the headhunter's "client" while you are merely the "candidate." The role of the headhunter is NOT to help you find a job; it is to help his or her client successfully fill a position. The headhunter always works for the employer and is paid to tend to the client's interest. The headhunter is not your pal, nor your therapist. This is a business relationship, so the information you choose to share is critical to how you will be presented to her client.

Network! Network! Network!

The true purpose of networking during a job search is to get information, insights and introductions. But you must think strategically. Who has the information you need? Who can introduce you to someone on your target list? Whose guidance and counsel do you trust? If the only question you pose to your contacts is "do you know of any job openings," the answer is likely to be "no, but I'll keep you in mind if I hear of anything." You must ask better questions to get better answers.

Identify WHO Can Help

The first step in the process is to prepare a list of people with whom to network. Think about your Board of Advisors, family members, friends, classmates, co-workers, professors, managers (past/present), service industry professionals (doctors, lawyers, accountants), professionals in the field. Consider all the people you know: commuter buddies, your children's friends' parents, people from your gym or religious institution. Then consider all the people they know. Add to the list every day. Keep track of who referred you and how people are connected to each other.

Decide <u>WHAT</u> You Want From Each Contact

You need to have a clear objective about what you are trying to accomplish before you contact anyone on your list. **Think through your strategy first.** Why have you selected this person to contact? What information do you hope to learn? To whom can they introduce you? There should be no mystery or hidden agenda as to the purpose of the conversation. Consider the following sample approaches to potential contacts:

To a geographic contact: *"You have lived in this city for so long and know almost everyone..."*

To a socially active friend: *"You have so many friends, you probably hear about things before anyone..."*

To someone who works in your field: *"You've been working in the same type of job I am looking for, I am sure you have some idea how my skills might be viewed..."*

To a professor: *"You know better than anyone what kinds of jobs are open in this field..."*

To anyone you admire: *"You always seem to have good ideas..."*

To someone you have helped: *"We have helped each other in the past, so I am hoping you can help me now..."*

It is important to understand what you can reasonably expect from professional relationships and what is outside those bounds. It is reasonable to expect:

- information
- referrals to others who can help you
- reactions to your ideas and theories
- assistance in formulating plans
- feedback about resumes, cover letters and approach
- moral support

It is NOT reasonable to expect A JOB will be handed to you.

Most people do not know of many current job openings. If the first and only question posed to your contacts is *"Do you know of any openings?"* you will more often than not receive a NO and an opportunity may be lost. By asking questions like *"What do you do and what alternatives are out there?"* or *"Where do you see someone with my skills fitting in?"* or *"Do you know anyone who works at X?"* you will uncover information that will eventually generate opportunities and preserve your relationships.

It is important not to limit your efforts to only those with influential positions and the power to hire you. Remember, networking should only be used as a communication process to acquire information, NOT as a manipulation used to acquire power and influence over others. If you are playing the "advice and information game" when you really believe networking is nothing more than the back door route to a new position, you are being insincere, misleading and you will not be effective. People who are close to your level of experience and even those junior to you or in support positions can be great sources of information. Be nice to everyone along the way.

Job seekers are hesitant about "using" people or asking for help. Many people these days consider it foolish <u>not</u> to use contacts, and those in a position to help you might even be insulted that they were not asked for assistance. People <u>like</u> to help others. It makes them feel good, powerful and important. If you are doubtful, consider whether you would be willing to share your knowledge or give names to friends or business associates in order to be helpful. When you establish a specific and relevant basis for a conversation—ask for ideas, opinions, a reaction to your own thoughts—there is no reason for you to be turned down. Ask for something specific, something your contact can easily do.

EXERCISE: Categorize Your Contacts

List 30 people you believe might be able to assist you in your job hunt and consider how each can help. Divide the list into three categories:

A—those in a position to hire (this category may be very small);
B—those in a position to introduce you to others in a position to hire;
C—those with information or ideas

1. _____   4. _____

2. _____   5. _____

3. _____   6. _____

7. _____	19. _____
8. _____	20. _____
9. _____	21. _____
10. _____	22. _____
11. _____	23. _____
12. _____	24. _____
13. _____	25. _____
14. _____	26. _____
15. _____	27. _____
16. _____	28. _____
17. _____	29. _____
18. _____	30. _____

Learn **HOW** to Network

It is one thing to understand the concept of networking. It is quite another to know HOW to do it. The good news is networking is a learnable skill. Start with the easy ones, those friends and colleagues you feel comfortable calling. Invite them to lunch and say, *"I'm thinking about making a job change and wanted to bounce some ideas off you."* During these initial meetings you will begin to become more comfortable talking about yourself, and, because these are your friends, they will be more forgiving if you stumble slightly as you craft your message.

For people you do not know as well, use this four-step process: (i) a written approach letter or e-mail, (ii) follow-up phone call, (iii) informational interview and (iv) follow-up thank-you note.

i. Written Approach

Send a letter or e-mail to ask for <u>15</u> minutes of their time for <u>advice</u>. Do not put pressure on the individual to find you a job or to interview you. That may be a long-term result, but at this point, an informative conversation should be your objective.

LETTER OF INTRODUCTION

Your Name

Street Address
City, State zip
Date

Contact Name
Title
Organization
Street Address
City, State zip code

Dear :

Jack O'Neill suggested that I contact you about my interest in career opportunities in employment law (the legal community in New Jersey, etc). I am a graduate of XYZ Law School with 4 years' experience in ...

(Your next paragraph should tell something about your background. Include your prior work experience, skills, interests, academic history, connection to the geographic region, etc. Your goal is to pique the reader's interest.)

I hope to benefit from the experience and knowledge of others in the field (in New Jersey) who might advise me on opportunities for someone with my qualifications. I would appreciate the opportunity to meet with you for 15 minutes for your guidance. I will call your office next week to see if we can schedule a meeting.

I look forward to discussing my plans with you.

Sincerely,

Your Name

LETTER OF REINTRODUCTION

Your Name

Street Address
City, State zip
Date

Contact Name
Title
Organization
Street Address
City, State zip code

Dear :

It was a pleasure meeting you last week at _____. (Remind your contact where you met and the nature of your conversation. Restate your interest in the topic.)

(Your next paragraph should tell something about your background. Include your prior work experience, current situation, skills, interests, academic history, connection to the geographic region, etc. Your goal is to pique the reader's interest.)

I would appreciate the opportunity to further discuss my career development strategies with you in order to benefit from your expertise. I will call your office next week to see if we can schedule a 15-minute meeting.

(Close with some reference to your prior conversation.) Enjoy the Opera next week.

Thank you again for your help.

Sincerely,

Your Name

Do **NOT** include your resume with the letter. The receiver may assume you are applying for a job and may not bother to read the letter, thereby missing your request. Simply supply any relevant information contained in your resume in paragraph two of the letter.

If you prefer to e-mail your contact, keep in mind that while less formal than a letter, an e-mail is still a business correspondence. You should use a salutation. Grammar, spelling and proper punctuation are important. Create a secure e-mail address separate from your current work address. Yahoo and Hotmail offer free e-mail accounts. Make sure to select a professional name. All job search–related inquiries should come from this address.

ii. Follow-up Telephone Calls

Nothing is more effective than a well-written correspondence followed promptly by a telephone call. If you sent a letter, call 5-7 days later; for an e-mail, follow up 2-3 days later. The telephone is the most underutilized tool available to the job seeker. Most job seekers never even try to call decision-makers and even those who do, do not do so often enough. By using the telephone, job seekers can reduce uncertainty and waiting time. It is your responsibility as the job seeker to make the telephone call and schedule a meeting.

Prepare a script so you can clearly and succinctly introduce yourself and articulate your request. Your ability to present yourself and explain what you hope to gain from meeting with your contacts will determine their response to you. Why have you chosen this particular organization and, more importantly, this particular person to contact over all of the other possibilities? What specifically do you want to find out? These types of questions will help you to clarify your objectives in networking before you call or write contacts and will increase your chances of piquing their interest in meeting you. You must be prepared to say more than "I have just lost my job and I was wondering if you know of any openings." Consider instead:

> *"Hello, Mr./Ms. _____. This is Sally Smith. I am calling at the suggestion of Jack O'Neill. I sent you a letter last week explaining... (restate the first paragraph of your letter) and I was wondering if you might have 15 minutes next Tuesday or Thursday to meet with me?"*

Remember, you do not want to exert pressure on people to find you a job. You only want to explain the purpose of the meeting and articulate how you believe your contacts can be helpful. The objective is to unearth information about them and their job experience.

Choose a private, comfortable setting for making calls. Besides your script, keep a pen, pad and copy of your resume and letter at hand. Being prepared will help to ameliorate an attack of phone fright and will prevent you from omitting important information. Your script should include:

- whom you are calling (address the person by name)
- who referred you
- why you are calling (to determine the status of your letter)
- how you believe the person could be helpful

Your introduction should be brief, listener directed and upbeat. As the example suggests, consider giving the listener a choice between something and something, not a choice between something and nothing. For example: *"I was wondering if we might meet Tuesday afternoon or Thursday morning"* is more effective than *"I was wondering if we might meet next week."* Even if both Tuesday and Thursday are not convenient, offering a choice avoids complete rejection and steers the interviewer into discussing timing. Remember to confirm time and exact address, including floor and room number.

If people seem hesitant to grant your request to meet, clearly state that you are not looking for a job with them and that you are only looking for advice and information. For example:

Reluctant Contact: *"I really don't know of any openings. I'm not sure I can help you."*

Your Response: *"I appreciate your candor. At this point in my job search, I'm just trying to talk to as many people in the field as possible to get some feedback on my approach and brainstorm where possibilities may exist. I would appreciate it if you could spare 10 minutes for me. Does next Tuesday or Thursday work for you?"*

Suspicious Contact: *"If you are looking for a job you should contact HR."*

Your Response: *"Actually, I am not looking for a job at the moment, although I'd be happy to contact HR at a later day. Right now I am eager to meet as many people in the field as possible to get some feedback* *on my approach and brainstorm where possibilities may exist. I would be grateful if you could spare 15 minutes for me. Does next Tuesday or Thursday work for you?"*

Negative Contact: *"I can't help you. I'm not the person you should talk to."*

OR

"I don't have time to meet with you."

Your response: *Thanks for your candor. Could you suggest someone else I should talk to? Would it be ok if I used your name?*

If you are still met with resistance, politely bring the conversation to a close and than write a nice thank-you letter, again stating your intended purpose. Mention your disappointment in not being able to learn from the person's experience and ask to be remembered for future reference. Enclose your resume with this letter.

Perhaps the greatest challenge when using the telephone is reaching your target. The advent of voice mail has frustrated many job seekers. Be prepared to leave a detailed but short message of why you are calling and state a time when you will call back to alert your contact. **Do not simply leave a name and a phone number and expect a person to return your call.**

"Hello, Mr./Ms. _____. This is Sally Smith. I am calling at the suggestion of Jack O'Neill. I sent you a letter last week explaining... (restate the first paragraph of your letter) and I was hoping to arrange a time to meet with you. I'll call back this afternoon at 3 pm. If that time is not good for you and you would prefer to call me back, I can be reached at 212-555-2222. Thank you and I look forward to speaking with you."

Be sure to speak slowly and clearly, especially when leaving your phone number.

Reaching receptionists or secretaries can provide a unique set of problems. Keep in mind that it is part of their job to screen phone calls. Secretaries are trained to keep the unwanted world away from a busy boss.

Try to take control of the conversation from the beginning, following your script. Sound confident. If requested to give a reason for the call, offer,

"She is expecting my call. We have corresponded," or *"I am calling at the suggestion of Mr. Smith."* If your voice conveys uncertainty, you may be giving the secretary just cause to screen you out. NEVER try to deceive the secretary by saying, *"I am a friend,"* or *"it is a personal call."* You will only alienate your prospect.

Secretaries can be your best allies or among your biggest stumbling blocks. Be sure to get their name and establish friendly relationships. Remember, they have access to your target and are likely to share their impressions of you with the boss.

If you doubt that your target will return your call, indicate that you are going out and ask when might be a good time to call again. If after several calls, none have been returned, do not signal exasperation. This will make the secretary defensive. Instead, apologize for calling so often. Ask if you could schedule a phone appointment to break the cycle of telephone tag. The secretary may be moved by your respect for her time and either schedule a phone appointment or provide you with information about a better time to call, or, at least, place your message at the top of the pile.

If you cannot get the cooperation of the secretary, try calling before 9 a.m., after 5 p.m. or during lunch when your target person is more likely to answer his/her own phone. Busy lawyers are also likely to be in their offices on weekend days.

Understand that it may take several attempts over a period of weeks—even months—to get someone's attention. Keep in mind that the way to get a response to any kind of marketing communication is to create multiple, <u>positive</u> impressions.

iii. The Informational Interview

Once you are in your contact's office, it is your responsibility to lead the conversation. You should be prepared to:
- explain the purpose of the meeting
- show how your contact can be helpful
- present your background and skills to put the meeting in context
- ask questions to elicit the information you need
- present a pleasant, positive demeanor
- get the names of others who could be helpful
- be considerate of their time

The purpose of the meeting is to determine how your skills and talents could be used in different settings, so it is important to do a good job presenting them. The ability to communicate your qualifications to potential employers entails more than just informing them of your technical competence. You must be able to illustrate that you have the requisite personal attributes—things like problem-solving abilities, analytical skills, assessment and planning capabilities—to perform the job. The examples you use to talk about your accomplishments should elucidate your thinking and problem-solving style. The more concrete and specific you are, the better able your contact will be to think of possibilities for you and suggest additional people you should meet. It is critical that job seekers engage in the self-assessment process <u>before</u> they launch into the networking process.

A common mistake people make when job prospecting is to use the meeting as a therapy session. You do not want to inspire guilt, pity or dread. Your goal should be to make your contacts feel good about their ability to help you. It is important that you present yourself as positive, confident and self-assured, not negative, needy and desperate. Never make your contacts feel sorry for you or responsible for your situation. Do not scoff at their suggestions by saying "I've tried that and it does not work"; otherwise your contacts will doubt their ability to help and begin to avoid you. If you need to express anger, bitterness, anxiety, etc., talk to a career counselor or seek out a member of the clergy or a sympathetic friend before meeting with your contacts.

During your appointments you may want to address:

A. The careers of the people you are visiting:
   - their background
   - how their interest developed in this area
   - what they like best/least about their work
   - their "career steps" (what former jobs they held, what they learned from each, how they progressed from one job to the next)

B. Advantages and disadvantages of working with that:
   - type of firm, agency or corporation
   - type of law practice
   - geographical area

C. The structure of their organization and how it operates:
   - whom they supervise, and to whom they report
   - performance expectations
   - advancement opportunities
   - future growth potential

D. Characteristics the organization values in an employee.

E. Advice regarding how to make yourself an attractive candidate including suggestions on:
- upgrading your resume
- interviewing techniques
- additional educational and experiential qualifications you might pursue
- where to go to find more information
- others in the field with whom you could speak

F. Information about any specific job openings you should consider

Once contacts get to know you, and you have asked questions about their career (showing genuine interest), it is their prerogative to offer further assistance. Towards the conclusion of your talk, their thoughts might naturally turn to what action they might take on your behalf.

You should express gratitude for offers of assistance and take notes if individuals suggest that you contact colleagues. You might add, *"Would it be OK if I use your name when contacting this person?"* If your contacts offer to send out your resumes for you or make calls on your behalf, make sure you arrange to get a list of those contacted so that you can take control of the follow-up process. Assuming responsibility for the follow-up process will allow your contacts to experience you as efficient and conscientious.

If your contacts do not offer assistance or additional names of people to call, you might gently ask if they could suggest names of individuals to speak to who could give you more information.

You may find that the 15 minutes you asked for stretched to a conversation lasting an hour or more. This usually occurs because people are flattered that you came to them for advice, and are asking about things of importance to them. However, it's up to <u>you</u> to stick to your preset time limit, and let your contacts take the initiative to extend the meeting, if desired.

People love to talk about themselves. This type of conversation tends to be very warm and animated, filled with good will. Even though they may not know of a specific job opening, your contacts are likely to keep you in mind when they do have one, or when colleagues are trying to fill a position, they may recommend you to them.

When you meet with people on your network list, take notes about the meeting. It would be helpful to start a file for each contact. Whether you choose a sophisticated computer software program or a simple 3 x 5 index card filing system, be sure to include:

- the contact's name (be sure you have the correct spelling)
- the date of the contact
- the results of the meeting
- follow-up that is required and the timeframe
- the person who referred you
- any personal information that may be helpful
- your impressions of the person and the organization

The job search process requires that you continually make phone calls, schedule appointments, write follow-up notes, contact new people, etc. It is important to record the dates and times for each activity on a pocket calendar to remind you what needs to be done. This will help to organize your days, which in turn will allow you to get more accomplished. (See Chapter Six.)

Sample

Name phone/email	Date of Initial Contact	Results of Meeting	Follow-up Action Required	Referrals	Personal Info	Impressions

iv. Follow-up Correspondence

When someone has taken the time to meet with you to provide information, advice and support, it is necessary and appropriate to send a thank-you note shortly after the meeting. While an e-mail is ok, a handwritten note—in the form of a note card or on your personal stationery—is better. Your message should convey gratitude for the time, attention and guidance shared.

People who help you should be kept apprised of your job search. Remember, the way to get a response to any kind of marketing communication is to create multiple, positive impressions. YOUR job search may not be the most important thing on your contact's mind. If you occasionally can remind people that you are still in the job search, other opportunities may present themselves down the line.

It is appropriate to reconnect with people to:

1) Update and inform. Reconnect with contacts periodically to update them on your job search activities or when new information arises. For example, if your contacts connect you to someone in their network, let them know how the meeting went. Or, if you were just admitted in a new jurisdiction, let them know. Keeping people up to speed is helpful, but don't overdo it. Only contact people if there is truly something of significance to report. If you find yourself calling or e-mailing more than once a week, you have wandered into the "pest" zone. Also, don't worry if your contact does not respond to your e-mail or if you do not speak with the person directly. Leave a **brief** voicemail message with the pertinent information. Don't ask them to return your call. Your goal is to minimize the amount of time and attention you ask of people. Your objective is simply to stay on their radar screen. If you haven't had a reason to connect, touch base every 4-6 weeks to check in. "Wanted to see if you've heard anything."

2) Solicit information and advice. Call contacts with simple questions. "I just scheduled an interview with "X" and was wondering if you might have 5 minutes to share any insights you might have." These types of solicitation should definitely not be made too often and the questions/guidance should be specific and in instances when their opinion would definitely make a difference. If you are considering asking them which tie to wear to the interview, you are wasting their time.

3) Share information of interest to THEM. Your job search activities may uncover information that may be of interest to your contacts. Perhaps you will learn information about emergent trends, client development opportunities or something of a personal nature. Make those connections whenever possible.

Finally, remember you want your contacts to always have a pleasant, positive experience during their interactions with you so that they will be inspired to refer you to people. It is NEVER appropriate to call your contacts to whine or complain. While the job search can be frustrating, use your friends and family or hire a career counselor to help you through the rough patches, NOT your contacts. Most importantly, remember to let your contacts know when you have landed a position. Thank them again for their support and guidance and offer your willingness to return the favor.

After each informational interview, review your performance. Did you present your skills as effectively as possible? Did you craft your questions to elicit the information you needed? What could you have done better?

Organize the information you have received. Are there new books to read, new resources to consider, additional organizations to explore, new people to meet? Develop your plan of action based on this new information. (See Chapter Six.)

Informational interviewing requires a long-term view, strategic planning and a commitment to working at it. It takes patience and perseverance to use this process to uncover job opportunities, but it is the most effective method to find a professional job.

Summary

The internet is a powerful tool filled with useful information. When it is used in conjunction with old-fashioned methods like reviewing newspaper ads and relying on headhunters as well as networking, you will have the necessary fuel to get you to your final destination quickly.

Draw Your Own Map

Create Winning Resumes, Cover Letters and Deal Sheets

Marketing materials are necessary to launch your job search. Your self-marketing kit should contain a resume, cover letter, writing sample, transcripts, references, recommendations and a deal sheet or list of significant cases.

Draft Your Resume

Let's start with the resume. Think of it as a sales document. To design an effective sales document, you must have a clear idea of the job you are seeking so that you can skew your resume to your target audience. That is why we have spent so much time concentrating on self-assessment and market research. Ideally, you created a resume file early in your career, adding experiences and accomplishments as they occurred. But even if you have not, now is as good a time as any to begin. First, decide which information to include; pay close attention to the words you use to describe your experiences. Then, concentrate on the format and style you want to use to best display your content.

Your resume is an opportunity to create a positive impression with an employer. Because this document is a self-portrait, it is difficult to give generic advice on the preparation of a legal resume. Yet, there are key concepts and general rules of thumb to follow concerning format and content.

- A resume should be brief. Conventional wisdom suggests resumes should be one page long. However, if you have had an extensive career, you do yourself a disservice by eliminating relevant information or cramming your content into one page. Expand to a second page. Make sure the second page is at least half full, with your name at the top.

- Name, address, phone number and e-mail should appear at the top of the resume—Phone numbers are essential; invest in an answering machine to avoid missed opportunities. Your message should be clear, professional and preferably in your voice. Also, be sure to have a professional e-mail address.

- A **JOB OBJECTIVE** is not necessary. However, you might want to consider a **CAREER SUMMARY**, which highlights your professional background as it relates to the position you are seeking. It should consist of several statements that demonstrate your skills and credentials. The focus is on your abilities. Describe what you can do, not what you want to do.

- **EXPERIENCE** section can be formatted either **Chronologically or Functionally. Chronological resumes** are oriented by date, with the most recent position first and proceeding backward. This is the most popularly used and accepted format because it is logical and easy to follow. This is the format to use if you have a steady work history with no gaps and if your most recent job is related to your job target. If you have a substantial work history, consider adding **Accomplishments** under each entry to focus the reader on your successes. If you are switching directions, a **functional resume** may be more effective. Here accomplishments and experience are organized under broad practice area or skills headings with the most important category (to the potential employer) at the top, followed by two or three other functions. This format allows you to organize your experience according to your talents. It also allows you to de-emphasize employment dates, company names and titles, which should be included under the heading Employment.

- **EDUCATION** section should contain all pertinent information from your law school experience, including the official name of the school, year of graduation, Journal/moot court experience and a list of any appropriate academic and/or extracurricular activities. This section should also contain similar information for other graduate schools attended as well as your undergraduate institution. If you have attended an Ivy League school, consider leading with the Education section. If you had stellar grades in law school, you may also want to keep your education section first for your first year or two after graduation. Otherwise your education should go <u>after</u> experience on a legal resume once you have graduated from law school.

- **BAR STATUS** <u>can be handled a variety of ways</u>. It can be listed as a separate heading or under Career Summary.

- <u>Consider including a section that draws attention to unique skills such as foreign languages or personal interests</u>. The section may be titled **PERSONAL** or **INTERESTS**. Its purpose is to facilitate conversation or "break the ice" during an interview and to give the employer a more well rounded appreciation of your background. Make sure that your personal interests are descriptive—e.g., *"travel to the Far East, Mexican cooking and nineteenth century literature"* are much more effective than *"travel, reading and cooking."*

- <u>Also consider adding a section for</u> **PROFESSIONAL AFFILIATIONS** <u>and/or</u> **COMMUNITY ACTIVITIES**. This will enable you to list bar association committees, board memberships, pro bono work, and any other extracurricular or leadership positions on your resume.

- <u>You can include CLE or other continuing legal education courses or symposia under a</u> **CONTINUING LEGAL EDUCATION** <u>section</u>. This can be useful to include if you are trying to make a transition to a different practice area. You can demonstrate knowledge of and an interest in a particular field by listing this type of coursework on your resume.

- <u>Legal resumes should generally be CONSERVATIVE IN APPEARANCE.</u> As much as you may be tempted to stand out from the pack, the legal profession is conservative, and flashy "ploys" are not usually well received. White, off-white or cream colored heavy stock paper should be used. No photos or other graphics are necessary. Ten, eleven or twelve point type size is appropriate. Good fonts include TIMES NEW ROMAN and ARIAL.

- <u>No Personal Information (height, weight, age, marital status, health)</u> need appear on your resume.

- <u>Prepare a list of References</u> that is separate from your resume. It is not appropriate on a legal resume to include names of references. It is, however, a good idea to prepare a separate sheet of paper listing references (three is usually an adequate number) to have available when you go in for an interview. Don't forget to alert your references first so they are prepared for a potential employer's call. Phone references are usually preferred over written references.

Other tips and techniques to keep in mind:

- Use CAPITALIZATION, **bold print,** *italics,* <u>underlining,</u> indentation and outline format to present information. Make it easy for the reader to scan. Make sure the overall look is neat and clean.

- Use generous margins (but not so generous as to look skimpy.). Balance the text on the page.

- Put dates on the right hand margin instead of the left so they do not stand out to the point that the employer will be distracted from the more important aspects of your resume.

- Use "bullets" if your descriptions are longer than 5 lines.

- Use strong action verbs to describe experience and accomplishments. Be specific.

- Proofread to eliminate errors and typos.

Once you have created your resume, you need to ensure it translates properly via e-mail. Send it to a few friends to make sure it opens properly and that there are no formatting issues. (For example, you may need to eliminate headers/footers.) You could also use the *Save As* function on your computer to create a second version of your resume in ASCII text or Rich Text Format. These are easier to use when posting resumes in online databases. Proofread the new document to be sure information translated properly during the reformatting process. Finally, recognize that some employers, fearful of computer viruses, may not accept e-mails with attachments. In those instances send your resume as the text of an e-mail message.

EXERCISE: Resume Worksheets

Use these worksheets to compile all the information for each category. Include EVERYTHING. You may ultimately decide not to include certain information on the resume, but do not edit at this stage. It may be worth including a college internship or long since past experience if it is relevant or uniquely interesting.

EDUCATION (Include the official names of the schools, years of graduation, and a list of any appropriate academic and/or extra-curricular activities.)

EXPERIENCE (Include legal and non-legal, full-time and part-time positions. Compile the information chronologically. You can decide later how to format the information on the resume.)

ACCOMPLISHMENTS (Include significant deals or matters you have worked on. List by transactions, practice area or industry.)

PROFESSIONAL AFFILIATIONS (List Bar Association Committees, Board Memberships, industry groups, etc.)

COMMUNITY ACTIVITIES (List pro bono activities, community groups, volunteer work, etc.)

PERSONAL (List unique skills or interests.)

Skill Identification Action Verbs

accelerate	argue	change	convince
accept	arrange	check	coordinate
accomplish	articulate	chose	copy
account for	assess	classify	correct
achieve	assist	clear up	counsel
acquire	assume	close	count
act	assure	coach	craft
activate	attend	combine	create
adapt	author	communicate	critique
add	authorize	compare	dance
adjust	award	complete	deal
administer	balance	compose	debate
advise	begin	conceive	decide
advocate	bolster	conceptualize	define
aid	boost	conclude	delegate
alphabetize	brief	condition	delineate
alter	budget	conduct	deliver
analyze	build	confront	demonstrate
anticipate	calculate	consolidate	describe
apply	care	construct	design
appoint	catalog	consult	designate
appraise	caught	continue	detail
approach	cause	contract	determine
arbitrate	chair	control	develop

devise	focus	innovate	nurture
diagnosis	forecast	inspect	observe
digest	foresee	instruct	open
diminish	formulate	insure	operate
direct	forward	interpret	order
discover	foster	interview	organize
display	frame	introduce	originate
distill	gain	investigate	overcome
draft	gather	join	oversee
dramatize	generate	joke	pace
draw	give	judge	paint
earn	grab	juggle	participate
educate	grade	know	perceive
elect	grasp	labor	perform
elicit	greet	launch	persist
employ	gross	lead	persuade
encompass	guide	learn	photograph
encourage	handle	lecture	pioneer
enjoy	hasten	license	place
enlarge	heighten	listen	plane
enlist	help	lobby	play
ensure	highlight	locate	police
enter	hike	look	position
establish	hire	maintain	practice
estimate	house	make	prepare
evaluate	hunt	manage	present
excel	hypothesize	map out	prevail
execute	identify	master	process
exercise	illustrate	maximize	produce
expand	imagine	meet	profit
experiment	implement	modify	program
explain	improve	monitor	prohibit
explore	improvise	motivate	project
extrapolate	include	move	promote
facilitate	incorporate	name	prove
familiarize	increase	neaten	publicize
figure	indicate	negotiate	publish
file	inform	net	purchase
finance	initiate	notice	qualify

quantify	review	state	transfer
quicken	revise	stop	transform
quote	save	straighten	translate
rate	scout	streamline	travel
read	screen	strengthen	treat
realize	script	strip	tutor
receive	scrutinize	study	type
recognize	select	submit	uncover
recommend	sell	suggest	understand
record	send	summarize	undertake
recreate	serve	supervise	unearth
recruit	set	support	unfurl
refine	ship	surmount	update
reflect	show	survey	utilize
relate	sift	tailor	value
remember	simplify	target	venture
renovate	sing	teach	verbalize
repair	solve	test	view
report	sought	theorize	visualize
represent	spearhead	think	welcome
rescue	specify	tighten	win
research	speech write	tour	work
respond	speaking	track	write
return	stage	train	
reveal	start	transcribe	

Cluster Transferable/Functional Skills

Administrative	Creative	Financial	Problem-Solving
bookkeeping	design	accounting	analyze
classify	develop	administer	decide
collect	establish	allocate	diagnose
compile	illustrate	audit	examine
compute	imagine	balance	execute
examine	improvise	budget	plan
file	invent	calculate	prove
organize	perform	forecast	reason
record	revitalizing	invest	recognize
word processing	visualize	project	validate

Communication	Management	Research	Technical
draft	advise	assess	adjust
edit	communicate	calculate	align
explain	coordinate	collect	assemble
influence	counsel	diagnose	draft
interpret	decide	evaluate	engineer
interview	delegate	examine	install
listen	direct	extrapolate	observe
mediate	lead	interview	operate
promote	negotiate	investigate	program
speak	persuade	synthesize	repair
translate	plan		
write	supervise		

		Selling	**Training**
		communicate	adapt
Human Relations	**Public Relations**	contact	communicate
advise	conduct	educate	demonstrate
assist	consult	inform	enable
counsel	inform	organize	encourage
empathize	plan	persuade	evaluate
facilitate	present	plan	explain
guide	promote	present	instruct
listen	represent	promote	plan
mentor	research	schedule	stimulate
motivate	respond		
represent	write		
serve			

Sample Resume Formats

STANDARD CHRONOLOGICAL FORMAT

NAME

                                                123 Main Street
                                                City, St
                                                212-555-1212
                                                jdoe@hotmail.com

BAR STATUS
Admitted in New York and Connecticut (or) Passed New York State Bar; awaiting admission

LEGAL EXPERIENCE
   Employer Name   City, St
   <u>Your Title</u>   Dates
   Description. Use action verb.

   Employer Name   City, St
   <u>Your Title</u>   Dates
   Description. Use action verb.

   Employer Name   City, St
   <u>Your Title</u>   Dates
   Description. Use action verb.

ADDITIONAL EXPERIENCE
   Employer Name   City, St
   <u>Your Title</u>   Dates
   Description. Use action verb.

   Employer Name   City, St
   <u>Your Title</u>   Dates
   Description. Use action verb.

EDUCATION
   School Name
   J.D., May 1996
   Class Standing: Top 1/3
       Honors:
       Activities:

   School Name
   B.A., Economics May 1993
   Class Standing: Top 1/3
       Honors:
       Activities:

LANGUAGES
   Fluent in Spanish; working knowledge of German

PERSONAL
   Interests include spy novels, cross-country skiing and hockey.

REFERENCES AVAILABLE UPON REQUEST

CHRONOLOGICAL FORMAT—Two Pages

NAME
Address
Phone
E-mail

LEGAL EXPERIENCE:

XYZ COUNTY DISTRICT ATTORNEY'S OFFICE   August 1991 – Present

Trial Counsel: Lead prosecutor of infanticides and neonaticides in office of 400 attorneys. Caseload also includes homicides, child and adult rape and sodomy, domestic violence, child abuse and narcotics investigations, as well as the handling of numerous high-profile cases. Extensive courtroom experience in presenting and cross-examining experts in DNA, serology, fingerprint identification, ballistic and chemical analysis, forensic pathology, psychiatry, psychology and various other medical issues.

Supervisor: Advise and direct federal, state and local law enforcement officials in homicide and complex felony cases from crime scene management through investigation protocol and trial.

Instructor: Develop and teach curriculum for in-house accredited Continuing Legal Education Program on felony trial preparation and technique.

UNITED STATES ATTORNEY'S OFFICE
SOUTHERN DISTRICT OF NEW YORK   December 1989 – June 1990

Intern: Researched and drafted memoranda of law; assisted in witness preparation for U.S. v. XYZ.

TEACHING EXPERIENCE:

LECTURER/INSTRUCTOR – Legal Professionals
 · Selected as adjunct instructor to develop and present nationwide curriculum on the prosecution of child fatalities; train junior to senior-level attorneys on all aspects of trial advocacy as well as faculty development for such programs.
 · Lecture on the prosecution of child abuse/neglect cases as well as the handling of high profile & media cases, for the Continuing Legal Education and Assistance Division of the New York State District Attorneys Association.
 · Design and deliver semi-annual instruction on summations, trial preparation and mock trial scenarios for newly hired prosecutors and police academy cadets.

NATIONAL CENTER FOR THE PROSECUTION OF CHILD ABUSE; AMERICAN PROSECU-
TORS RESEARCH INSTITUTE; NATIONAL DISTRICT ATTORNEYS ASSOCIATION;
NATIONAL COLLEGE OF DISTRICT ATTORNEYS; NEW YORK PROSECUTORS TRAIN-
ING INSTITUTE; NEW YORK CITY POLICE ACADEMY; NEW YORK STATE BASIC
PROSECUTORS COURSE

LECTURER/INSTRUCTOR – Medical Professionals
 · Moderate discussion on detection of child physical and sexual abuse within the emer-
gency room; educate third-year residents on trial preparation, testimonial and evidentiary issues.
 · Lecture physicians at an accredited Continuing Medical Education program on psychiatric and psychological defenses in the prosecution of child homicide cases.

CORNELL UNIVERSITY MEDICAL CENTER; WOODHULL PSYCHIATRIC & MEDICAL
CENTER; ST. BARNABAS HOSPITAL; MONTEFIORE MEDICAL CENTER

LECTURER/INSTRUCTOR – Law Students and Undergraduates
- Lecture on investigation and trial strategies in infanticide, neonaticide and child sexual and physical abuse cases.
- Instruct undergraduate students in Criminal Law, Civil Litigation, Contracts, Corporations, Immigration, Employment Law, Wills Trusts and Estates and Bankruptcy

COLUMBIA UNIVERSITY SCHOOL OF LAW; FORDHAM UNIVERSITY LAW SCHOOL; BROOKLYN LAW SCHOOL; HOFSTRA UNIVERSITY SCHOOL OF LAW; NEW YORK CAREER INSTITUTE (JUNIOR COLLEGE)

ADDITIONAL EXPERIENCE

20/20: ABC TELEVISION, *Legal Advisor*
Served as an ongoing advisor on various legal issues in child physical and sexual abuse cases. Provided guidance and background information as lead prosecutor for People v. ABC, a starvation/infanticide case featured on the program.

DISCOVERY CHANNEL, DOCUMENTARY
Featured subject and legal advisor for "Bronx County, Crime & Justice: Domestic Crime."

UNION HOSPITAL COMMUNITY HEALTH CENTER, *Board of Trustees*

INTERBORO INSTITUTE JUNIOR COLLEGE, *Board of Trustees*

EDUCATION:

XYZ SCHOOL OF LAW, New York
Juris Doctor, May 1991.

COLLEGE, New York
Bachelor of Arts in Sociology, May 1986.
Intercollegiate Varsity Football; Co-captain.

BAR ADMISSION:
New York State, 1992.
Southern and Eastern District Courts of New York, 1995.
United States Supreme Court, 2001.

REFERENCES AVAILABLE UPON REQUEST

CHRONOLOGICAL/ACCOMPLISHMENT FORMAT

Jane Doe
123 Main Street
Anywhere, USA 00000
212-555-1212
jdoe@hotmail.com

LEGAL EXPERIENCE:

ABC Law Firm New York, NY
Associate, M&A Practice Group 1999 – Present
- Represent corporations making strategic acquisitions and divestitures, and private equity groups making acquisitions and divestitures for their own account and for the account of funds that they sponsor.
- Structure transactions, draft and negotiate deal documentation, and plan, coordinate and supervise due diligence and transaction execution.
- Advise clients on tender offer rules and other securities law issues that arise in M&A transactions.
- Act as project manager and deal team coordinator. Manage, supervise and train junior and mid-level associates.

Accomplishments:
- ▶ Structured and drafted terms of convertible preferred stock of fourth largest Chapter 11 in U.S. history.
- ▶ Planned, coordinated and supervised due diligence, negotiated documentation and closed transaction voted *Deal of the Year* in category Product Mix (Europe) in *Asset Finance International.*

XYZ Law Firm New York, NY
Associate, Corporate Group 1995 – 1999
- Represent issuers and underwriters in a variety of transactions, including public and private debt and equity offerings, bank loans, securitizations, mergers and acquisitions, and tender and exchange offers.
- Lead multiple transactions, coordinating efforts of working groups and closing consistent with client goals.
- Conduct business and legal due diligence and draft related offering document disclosure.
- Research and resolve legal issues arising in capital markets and other transactions.

Accomplishments:
- ▶ Represented the underwriters in establishing the US$3.5 billion <u>Rule 144a/Regulation S Medium Term Note Program</u> of a Latin American media company.
- ▶ Represented a U.S beverage company in the <u>sale of its energy assets and its related merger and corporate reorganization.</u>
- ▶ Represented the underwriters in the 17.5 million share <u>common stock offering</u> of a U.S. energy company.

ADDITIONAL EXPERIENCE

Investment Bank New York, NY
Junior Trader, International Equities Trading 1989 – 1992
- Analyzed and examined international events for potential effects on equity markets and informed sales force of economic news, industry trends, and foreign exchange shifts.
- Provided consulting services to users to enhance existing business applications.
Computer Auditor, Internal Audit 1987 – 1989
- Provided consulting services to users to enhance existing business applications.

EDUCATION

Law School Name New York, NY
J.D., 1995 Top 10% of Class; Law Journal

College Name New York, NY
B.A., Economics, 1987

PROFESSIONAL ASSOCIATIONS and COMMUNITY SERVICE
Association of the Bar of the City of NY, Member, Corporation Law Committee
St. Mary's Church, Cantor
Girl Scouts of America, Troop leader

FUNCTIONAL FORMAT—GENERAL

Jane Doe
123 Main Street
Anywhere, USA 00000
212-555-1212
jdoe@hotmail.com

SUMMARY

Over fifteen years' litigation experience in state and federal courts. Strong skills in legal analysis and drafting, writing, fact expert depositions and oral arguments. Admitted in New Jersey (1989) and New York (1990)

PRACTICE AREAS

Environmental

Represent and advise on environmental liability and compliance obligations under CERCLA, RCRA, and ISRA. Represent clients in administrative and court proceedings regarding alleged Clean Water Act, ISRA, and RCRA violations. Represent clients on matters involving damage and insurance claims stemming from environmental contamination. Advise clients on issues including CERCLA, RCRA, TSCA, UST installation, operation and removal, Clean Water Act, Pollution Prevention Act, and Right-to-Know compliance and labeling obligations.

Employment

Primary responsibility for all aspects of employment litigation, including Title VII, ADA, ADEA, state discrimination laws, FMLA, whistleblower statutes, restrictive covenants, wage issues, in state and federal courts and administrative proceedings. Traditional labor representation of management includes grievance arbitrations, union elections, and unfair labor practices. Counseling on human resource issues.

Bankruptcy

Represent creditors, debtors, creditors' committees, trustees, plan proponents, receivers, assignees, and preference action parties in complex Chapter 11 cases and sophisticated workouts. Regularly appear before bankruptcy courts in the District of New Jersey and the Eastern and Southern Districts of New York.

General Litigation

Manage major complex litigations, involving CGL, D&O, E&O, Business Interruption, and Products Liability insurance coverage actions. Counsel and defend clients on products liability and intellectual property disputes. Represent clients in administrative challenges. Research and prepare bench memoranda, attend oral arguments and assist Judge in rendering opinions for the Court.

EXPERIENCE

Employer Name	City, State
Your Title	1998 – Present
Your Title	1995 – 1998
Employer Name	City, State
Your Title	1989 – 1995

The Honorable Chief Judge *Name*, United States Court of Appeals, Third Judicial Circuit
Law Clerk   1988 – 1989

EDUCATION

Law School Name	City, State
J.D., 1988 Top 10% of Class; Moot Court	
College Name	City, State
B.A., History and English, 1972	

PROFESSIONAL AFFILIATIONS

XXX County Superior Court, Mediator
NJ State Bar Association, Environmental Law Section, Chair

FUNCTIONAL FORMAT—TRANSACTIONAL

James Doe
123 Main Street
Anywhere, USA 00000
212-555-1212
jdoe@hotmail.com

SUMMARY
Senior Associate with eight years' transactional experience. Strong skills in legal analysis, drafting, negotiation. Admitted in New Jersey, New York and California.

PRACTICE AREAS
Corporate Securities

Advise companies regarding general corporate, governance, disclosure, stock exchange requirements and strategic matters. Facilitate compliance with Sarbanes-Oxley Act requirements. Negotiate matters on behalf of companies with the SEC, NYSE and other exchanges and regulatory entities. Draft annual, periodic, beneficial ownership and other SEC reports.

Cross-Border Transactions

Engage in corporate practice representing U.S., European and Latin American public companies and investment and commercial banks, in connection with cross-border corporate finance transactions. Draft and negotiate agreements in connection with project finance, securities offerings and structured finance transactions. Work jointly with international clients' legal, finance and audit departments in the implementation of internal control and disclosure procedures to ensure compliance with recent U.S. legislation.

Mergers & Acquisitions

Represent public and private companies in domestic and international mergers and acquisitions, private equity investments and joint ventures. Draft and negotiate limited liability company and limited partnership agreements. Advise clients on initial public offerings, sale of assets by entities under bankruptcy court protection and poison piles.

EXPERIENCE
Law Firm Name, LLP	New York, NY
Associate	1999 – Present
Law Firm Name, LLP	Los Angeles, CA
Associate	1995 – 1999
Summer Associate	Summer 1994

EDUCATION
Law School Name	Los Angeles, CA
J.D., 1995 Top 10% of Class; Law Journal	
College Name	Los Angeles, CA
B.A., History and English, 1992	

PROFESSIONAL ASSOCIATIONS

Association of the Bar of the City of NY, Member, Corporation Law Committee
Law School Alumni Association, Chair, Annual Fund Committee

References available upon request

FUNCTIONAL FORMAT—LITIGATION

Jane Doe
123 Main Street
Anywhere, USA 00000
212-555-1212
jdoe@hotmail.com

SUMMARY

Over fifteen years' litigation experience in state and federal courts. Strong skills in legal analysis and drafting, writing, fact expert depositions and oral arguments. Admitted in New Jersey (1989) and New York (1990)

PRACTICE AREAS

Environmental

Represent and advise on environmental liability and compliance obligations under CERCLA, RCRA, and ISRA. Represent clients in administrative and court proceedings regarding alleged Clean Water Act, ISRA, and RCRA violations. Represent clients on matters involving damage and insurance claims stemming from environmental contamination. Advise clients on issues including CERCLA, RCRA, TSCA, UST installation, operation and removal, Clean Water Act, Pollution Prevention Act, and Right-to-Know compliance and labeling obligations.

Employment

Primary responsibility for all aspects of employment litigation, including Title VII, ADA, ADEA, state discrimination laws, FMLA, whistleblower statutes, restrictive covenants, wage issues, in state and federal courts and administrative proceedings. Traditional labor representation of management includes grievance arbitrations, union elections, unfair labor practices. Counseling on human resource issues.

Bankruptcy

Represent creditors, debtors, creditors' committees, trustees, plan proponents, receivers, assignees, and preference action parties in complex Chapter 11 cases and sophisticated workouts. Regularly appear before bankruptcy courts in the District of New Jersey and the Eastern and Southern Districts of New York.

General Litigation

Manage major complex litigations, involving CGL, D&O, E&O, Business Interruption, and Products Liability insurance coverage actions. Counsel and defend clients on products liability and intellectual property disputes. Represent clients in administrative challenges. Research and prepare bench memoranda, attend oral arguments and assist Judge in rendering opinions for the Court.

EXPERIENCE

Law Firm Name, LLP	City, State
Equity Partner	1998 – Present
Litigation Associate	1995 – 1998
Law Firm Name, LLP	City, State
Litigation Associate	1989 – 1995
The Honorable Chief Judge *Name*	
United States Court of Appeals, Third Judicial Circuit	
Law Clerk	1988 – 1989

EDUCATION

Law School Name	City, State
J.D., 1988 Top 10% of Class; Moot Court	
College Name	City, State
B.A., History and English, 1972	

PROFESSIONAL AFFILIATIONS

XXX County Superior Court, Mediator
NJ State Bar Association, Environmental Law Section, Chair

REFERENCES AVAILABLE UPON REQUEST

Secure References and Recommendations

Ask people if they would be willing to serve as a reference before you give out their names and contact information. Even if someone has agreed in the past, it is important to check in with them again if some time has lapsed. The more your references understand about the job for which you are applying, the better able they will be to tailor their remarks in a favorable way. Have a conversation with your references and come to a mutual agreement as to what will be said. You can initiate this conversation and actually tell them, to some extent, what you would like them to say. They are likely to agree with any reasonable suggestion. Be prepared to provide them with a copy of your resume and a "cheat sheet" that underscores your skills and talents.

In many instances, firm policy will only permit the organization to confirm dates of employment. If this is the case, consider instead requesting a "testimonial" from a partner who has supervised your work. A testimonial is not an official firm position, but rather one professional commenting on the work product of another.

Craft Notable Cover Letters

An individual cover letter must accompany each resume you send out. Its purpose is to support your candidacy by supplementing the information set forth in your resume. A cover letter should:

- convince the reader that you are worth getting to know better.

- draw attention away from liabilities by addressing potential questions the resume may raise.

- emphasize salient achievements and accomplishments in greater depth than the resume does.

- introduce new sales material that is not included on your resume.

- demonstrate enthusiasm and knowledge of the industry.

A cover letter is the ideal place to focus on the specific skills you want to emphasize for a particular employer. Some general guidelines for writing good cover letters include:

- Use correct grammar, good sentence structure and standard business letter format. Use paper that matches your resume.

- State the purpose of your letter. If you are responding to an ad, indicate the source. If you are writing at the suggestion of a mutual acquaintance, indicate that immediately. If you are writing about the possibility of a job, indicate why you are writing to this particular organization. Cover letters should be slanted as individually as possible.

- Pinpoint how your skills and experience relate to the particular needs of the employer to whom you are writing. Focus your letter on the needs of the reader. Focus on what you can do for the employer. What credentials, skills and experience do you have that would help the employer? No one cares what the job would do for you.

- Always be objective when describing yourself to an employer. For example, instead of writing *"I am a hard worker," "I would be a great asset to your firm"* or *"I have many leadership qualities,"* show them by means of examples from your past: *"The experience I gained as director of the office is indicative of my leadership abilities."*

- Address your letter to a specific person by name and title.

- Limit your cover letter to three or four paragraphs. It should rarely be more than one page.

- Present unique or distinctive attributes, without using superlatives, in an attractive, professional and well-written manner.

- Close your cover letter with a request for an interview indicating what action you will take—i.e., that you will call them (within 7-10 days) to arrange a meeting. Then follow through.

- Keep careful records of the positions for which you have applied. Maintain copies of your correspondence with dates indicating when you will follow-up. FOLLOW-UP is crucial.

Sample Cover Letter

Your name
Street Address
City, State zip
E-Mail
Date

Employer Name
Title
Organization
Street Address
City, State zip

Dear :

First paragraph: Mention the name of any person who referred you to this employer first, if this information is available to include. Otherwise, start your letter with a powerful statement that will grab the reader's attention. Identify yourself and the type of position you are seeking. State how you heard about this job opening. ("As an attorney with 15 years' experience in the prosecutor's office, I am writing in response to your advertisement in the New York Times for litigators.")

Second paragraph: Explain why you are qualified for or interested in this particular position. Stress how you can benefit the employer and what you have to offer to them. Don't repeat word-for-word the text of your resume. Rather, highlight and embellish upon the most significant aspects of your background with regard to the particular employer. Consider using bullets to draw attention to your accomplishments.

Third paragraph: Restate your interest in the particular organization, and express your desire for an interview. State how the employer may contact you if your address and phone number are different from the information on your resume. You may also state that you will call to set up an appointment. If you are truly interested in this job, feel free to take the initiative.

Sincerely,

Type your name

Enclosure

Prepare Deal Sheets

Consider preparing a deal sheet or a list of significant case matters to include in your self-marketing packet. These can be organized chronologically, by practice area or by industry to highlight a specific expertise.

NAME
Address
Phone/E-mail

MAJOR TRANSACTIONS

CORPORATE FINANCE:

Represented Company ABC as issuer in the $533,000,000 secondary offering of 19,125,000 shares of its common stock.

Represented Company XYS as issuer in the $560 million 144A 8.125% Senior Subordinated Notes offering.

Advised client in connection with a tender offer and consent solicitation statement.

PRIVATE EQUITY:

Advised client on 4(2) private placement, which included drafting shelf registration statement on S-3 and registration rights agreement ("PIPES transaction").

Represented private equity firm in its recapitalization of its investment in a portfolio company.

OTHER

Provide corporate advice to client in Chapter 11 in connection with new charters, by-laws and registration rights agreements.

NAME Address Phone E-Mail

<u>**Significant Legal Matters**</u>

Employment Litigation Experience

Corporation (E.D. Pa. 1998-2003) – Lead defense counsel for company in case involving claims of sexual harassment, gender discrimination, hostile environment and constructive discharge. Handled all aspects of case, over a period of nearly five years, from initial pleading through settlement 3 days prior to trial.

Smith v .Corporation X (N.D. Cal. 2003) – Lead defense counsel in case of gender discrimination and retaliation under the California medical leave act for company that provides billing and collection services for credit card companies throughout the United States. Supervised co-counsel representing an individual defendant at client's expense and handled initial discovery through settlement in court-mandated mediation.

Jone v. XYZ County (E.D. Pa. 2003) – Lead defense counsel in case involving alleged violation of Americans with Disabilities Act. Worked with counsel representing counsel*{counsel representing counsel ok?}* in related Workmen's Compensation Claim to arrange settlement through insurance at no expense to County.

Employment Contract/Severance/Restrictive Covenant Negotiations

Doctors v. Hospital (2003-2004) – Assisted in negotiation of severance for terminated emergency room doctors and provided advice on labor and employment issues. Drafted complaint for non-settling doctor.

Manufacturing Company – Negotiated employment contract in context of litigation regarding enforcement of restrictive covenant by employee's former employer.

Sales Representative – Worked with employee's personal counsel in resolving disputes and avoiding litigation to enforce restrictive covenant that employee signed with former employer.

Traditional Labor Matters

Labor Injunctions – Drafted injunction papers to prevent disruption of mass transit service resulting from labor picketing. Assisted with courtroom argument and negotiations.

Union representation attempts – Defeated attempts to unionize clients' employees in various settings including public utility company, single site of multinational corporation with numerous unionized employees and small site of large company that had unions in other locations.

Unfair Labor Charges – Defended against various unfair labor practice charges arising in context of representation cases, as a result of grievance proceedings or during contract negotiations.

Other Litigation Experience

XYZ Corporation (1989-1999) – Handled eviction procedures and negotiations with retail tenants on behalf of owner of shopping malls.

Litigation by HUD (1998-1999) – Defended owner of several properties against alleged violations of HUD violations.

Summary

The purpose of your resume and cover letter is to present your skills and credentials in an appealing way that inspires the reader to want to meet you. Use the following checklist to ensure your resume is ready for distribution.

____ Overall appearance is attractive, interesting/compelling.

____ The layout looks professional, well typed and printed, good margins, use of white space, caps, headings.

____ Accomplishments and problem-solving skills are emphasized.

____ Generalities have been avoided, and descriptions provide specific information about experience, projects, products and quantities with numbers/percentages when possible.

____ Extraneous material has been eliminated.

____ Text is well-written and reader friendly.

____ All sentences and paragraphs start with strong skill verbs in the past tense.

____ Essential information is included (address, phone numbers, e-mail address, bar admissions and year of Law School graduation).

CHAPTER NINE

Changing Directions

Develop Effective Interview Skills

Interviewing is comparable to developing an oral argument; you present your "case" based on the evidence you uncovered during the self-assessment process.

The basic question in every interview is "Why should I hire you?" Your objective is to translate your skills and attributes into benefits for the *employer*. You must be able to verbalize *why* your strengths are of *value* to this specific employer. Do not expect your past experience to speak for itself; be prepared to state the obvious.

The recruiter's objective is to assess your credentials, form an impression about your personality and determine the degree to which your interests and background correspond with the employer's hiring needs. Your background and record of accomplishments are amplified or diminished in the eyes of the recruiter by the general impression you create. Again, this is not to suggest that form is more important than substance; however, you want to ensure that the form you present does not create any barriers that prevent the employer from experiencing your substance.

The first few minutes of the interview are crucial. Employers make up their mind about candidates very early. Your handshake must be firm and confident, your gaze steady, your appearance impeccable and your confidence apparent.

Throughout the interview, decision makers are searching for clues that address the following questions:

- Can you do the job?
- Do you interact with people easily?
- Are you easy to interview, confident and clear in your answers?
- Do you listen?
- Do you ask sensible questions?
- Are you likeable?

- Will you complement or disrupt the department?
- Do you demonstrate good judgment?

Understand Interview Techniques

Interviewers typically use one of four interviewing methods to learn about candidates. Understanding the differences among these interviewing styles and preparing a strategy to effectively deal with each of them will improve your chances for success.

1. Directive Interview. Short, precise questions designed to elicit specific information about your background and interests are asked. The questions are formulated from the contents of your resume. Strategy: Answers should be brief and should objectively emphasize concrete accomplishments. Be careful to be concise but do not fall into the trap of responding with monosyllabic yes or no answers.

2. Non-Directive Interview. The recruiter's intent is to get the candidate to do all the talking. This usually does not work to your advantage. Your goal should be to get the recruiter to do at least 50% of the talking. Strategy: Construct a narrative history of yourself in advance to enable you to make a clear, concise statement explaining your purpose at the interview. Attempt to draw the recruiter into the conversation by asking questions.

3. Stress Interview. This is perhaps the most difficult interview of all. Its purpose is to measure your poise and emotional stability. The recruiter tries to appear curt, argumentative and/or impatient, firing questions in rapid succession. The questions may be designed to bait you into a topical argument. Strategy: Remain patient and calm. Indicating annoyance, tension or nervousness serves no purpose. To avoid a debate, try to change the topic by asking a question. Remember, this type of interview is designed to rattle you.

4. Free-Wheeling Interview. This type of interview lacks any semblance of structure or direction. Since many attorneys have limited interviewing experience, they have no tactical plan. Strategy: Control the flow of the conversation by opening the interview with highlights of your accomplishments and then move directly into your own questions. This helps put the recruiter at ease and helps to focus him/her on your assets.

Develop Your Message

While it is natural to be nervous in interviews, your goal is to focus on your message, not on your nerves. Remember, you would not be approaching this meeting at all if you were not qualified for the position. Your thorough preparation has made you aware of both your strengths and your weaknesses. But remember, the interviewer is there to see what you <u>have</u> to offer, not to hear explanations about what you don't have. When you practice answering interview questions, eliminate all "nos," "nots," "didn'ts," "althoughs," "buts," and "howevers" from your speech. Rephrase your answers using positive speech forms. This will prepare you to speak about yourself in a positive light.

Think of at least three main points you want to make. Use concrete and clear examples that demonstrate these strengths. Focus on these identified strengths during the interview and present them with conviction and enthusiasm. Remember that the interviewer must be able to see and hear the enthusiasm that you wish to portray.

Try to anticipate the types of questions you will be asked and prepare multi-level responses. Write out your answers. Review and edit them. First, give a <u>brief</u> summary, akin to a verbal outline, covering all salient points. Second, pause to gauge the interest of the interviewer and give a more detailed description <u>if the interviewer seems interested</u> or asks you to go on. Be certain that your responses highlight your skills and abilities, demonstrate your knowledge and expertise and reflect your motivation and personality. Even if you believe it is obvious that you are highly qualified for the position, take time to collect your thoughts and think about your answers.

EXERCISE: Planning the Interview

Write out the answers to the following questions.

1. What are the three points I must make at some time during our conversation?

2. What are my most marketable skills, both legal and management?

3. What are the skills I most want to use in my next job?

4. What are the aspects (tendencies, interview abilities, comfort level, specific questions I am nervous about being asked) of the interview situation on which I most need to work? What is the question I am most afraid of being asked? How will I respond?

EXERCISE: Interview Prep Questions

Rehearse your answers to the following questions.

1. Tell me about yourself. (What they're really asking here is, "What in your background makes you a good candidate for this job?")

2. What are your long-range and short-range goals and objectives? (Be sure to make the connection between your goals and this job for which you're interviewing.)

3. What do you see yourself doing five years from now? (Again, tie your answer into the position available. Never, ever say you want to be doing something unrelated.)

4. What two or three accomplishments have given you the most satisfaction? Why? (Talk about specific deals/projects, especially if they are relevant to the position.)

5. In what ways do you think you can make a contribution to our firm/company?

6. In what sort of environment are you most comfortable? (Your favorite environment should be similar to that of the employer with whom you are interviewing.)

7. Why do you want to work with our company/firm? (Be specific. Show you've done your research. Make sure the interviewer knows that you understand the difference between lawyering at a firm vs. in-house, etc.).

8. What do you consider to be the strongest qualities in your personality and character? (List about 3 and relate them to the job opening.)

9. I see from your resume that you (play basketball <u>or</u> speak French <u>or</u> are interested in real estate, etc. This is <u>not</u> a statement where you answer "yes" or "no." Hear this as: <u>tell me more about</u> ....).

10. What else do you think I should know about you? (From your preparation beforehand you will have an additional strength or accomplishment that you'll want to highlight here. Don't say there isn't anything else. You're more exciting than that.)

Identify every question you dread being asked. Prepare a succinct answer for each. Practice saying the answer aloud. Go over each question and response repeatedly until you are desensitized to the stress each causes.

Ace the Interview

Before you walk in the door, obtain information about the employer from as many sources as possible. Knowing about things like areas of practice and client bases enables you to formulate intelligent questions. You do not want to waste valuable time asking questions that can easily be answered by reading the employer's brochure. The more information you have before the interview the better you will be able to make a convincing connection between your skills and the employer's needs.

Assemble your interview kit. It should contain:
- Firm resume
- Contact information/directions to interview

- Extra copies of your resume
- Transcripts
- Deal Sheets
- Reference list or letters

Expect the unexpected so that you will not get rattled if things do not go according to plan. Interviewers may change, you may meet more people than expected or client demands may affect the appointment time. And remember, every question counts. Something as innocent as, "Did you have any trouble finding us?" could start the interview off on a bad note if you carry on about traffic, bad directions, etc.

During the interview, you must:

- **Establish rapport**—In addition to tangible things such as a good, firm handshake and appropriate eye contact, there are additional items that develop rapport between people. These include friendliness and sincere interest in the interviewer, as well as warmth and responsiveness to the interviewer. You must become aware of body language. Be sensitive to cues of boredom. If the interviewer keeps looking down at your resume or out the window, bring the statement you are making to a close.

- **Listen carefully**—Try to hear the question behind the question and respond to the interviewer's concerns. Get the interviewer to talk about the position to uncover exactly what is being sought. This will enable you to illustrate how you can fill these needs.

- **Ask questions**—Remember, this is a conversation; there should be interaction. Ask technical questions to demonstrate your knowledge of the field and to show that you are already looking for solutions to the employer's problems. Do NOT ask about benefits, vacations, pensions and hours until you know you have an offer. However, be prepared to answer questions about salary and benefits if posed by the interviewer. (Refer back to page 69).

- **Get feedback**—Before the end of the interview, ask if you have the qualifications they are seeking. If not, now is the best time to find out so you can adjust your approach.

- **Take control of the follow-up process**—When interviewers indicate they will "let you know," ask if you can call on a specific day in the future. This may help to accelerate the decision-making process. Also, let them know if you have other offers.

- **Maintain a positive attitude**—Adopt a "have done—can do—will do" attitude. It is not always what you say that counts but <u>how</u> you say it. View anything negative as a challenge, an opportunity, and something exciting. Do not be apologetic about anything; handle your "Achilles' heel" factually and non-defensively.

You can help an inexperienced interviewer feel more comfortable by asking questions. Your prepared questions can demonstrate your knowledge of the field and your interest in the employer and provide the interviewer with an opportunity to relax by talking about something with which he/she is familiar. You can ask things like:

- "What do you see as the growth areas of the firm?"
- "What departments are likely to do well in the next few years?"
- "What criteria are used to evaluate performance?"

If you are interviewing for a non-legal position, ask things like:

- "What role does the position play in helping the company achieve its mission?"
- "What are the five most important duties?"
- "From a management perspective, what skills/attributes do you think are most important?"

If you believe negative assumptions are being made about you, confidently address the issue in order to eliminate the perceptions.

- "During other interviews, I have been asked about (my ability to accept supervision from someone younger than I am, or limited experience in X or my commitment to this geographic area), and we haven't talked about that yet."

By offering questions that allow the interviewer to relax and think about the answers, the interview becomes a freer exchange of information, which benefits all the parties involved. You will appear more confident and the interviewer will feel more comfortable in your presence and will be more likely to recommend you. Your questions should not convey an undue concern over salary or time off or any of the more mundane aspects of the job. Stay interested in important aspects such as challenge, responsibility and those that show a mature and forward-thinking mentality. The dollars-and-cents concerns can be ironed out after an offer has been made.

Deflect Discriminatory Questions

Hiring decisions tend to be based on somewhat subjective material. Unfortunately, trying to determine if someone "fits in" to a particular environment can lead to subtle forms of discrimination. While interviewers usually try to avoid asking personal questions, most want to know all they can about the applicants. Help them by providing information that you are comfortable with discussing and would like the interviewer to know. The information you volunteer about yourself will be different from what every other applicant offers and will help you stand out in the crowd. A word of caution: do not allow yourself to be lured into intimate chit-chat. Regardless of the kindness of the interviewer, <u>nothing</u> is "off the record." Keep your comments job related and, if you can complement your resume in any way by adding something, do it.

Applicants who are not aware of what questions should and should not be asked are more likely to be victims of discrimination. The general rule of thumb is, if the information is not specifically job related, it should not be asked.

Examples of potentially *sensitive*—though not necessarily *unlawful*—subjects include:

- name
- residence
- age
- birthplace
- military service
- references
- national origin
- sex
- marital status
- family size

- race
- color
- physical description
- physical condition
- photograph
- religion
- arrest record
- criminal record
- fraternal membership

HOW the question is posed can determine its lawfulness. For example, asking *"Are you a U.S. Citizen?"* or *"Where were you born?"* is different from asking you *"Are you authorized to work in the U.S.?"* Similarly, while it is acceptable for an employer to inquire *"Are you willing to relocate?"* it is not acceptable for him/her to attempt to infer the answer to that by asking *"Are you married?"*

In most states there are laws that render some questions illegal, the general results being that an employer should not ask:

- if the applicant has worked under another name;
- the maiden name of the wife or mother of the applicant;
- an applicant to take a pre-employment physical examination or to inquire about the nature and severity of physical or mental handicaps;
- about marital plans, arrangements for child care, current or anticipated pregnancy status;
- about the occupations of spouses, parents or siblings;
- for information relating to family background that may reveal race, ethnicity, religion, citizenship and/or national origin;
- about holidays observed or membership in clubs, churches and fraternities;
- about languages written, spoken or read unless the employer is specifically seeking to hire someone with that particular skill;
- for proof of age;
- for a photograph <u>prior</u> to the interview;

When you suspect an interviewer has lured you into a dangerous area, you have three response options.

1. <u>Answer the question</u>. Realize, however, that you are providing information that is not job related and you risk harming your candidacy by responding "incorrectly."

2. <u>Refuse to answer the question</u>. While you are in your rights to do so, you will probably alienate the employer and come across as uncooperative, confrontational and hostile. Not exactly the ideal description of a desirable applicant.

3. <u>Reframe the question</u>. Consider the intent of the question. In other words, try to hear the question behind the question. For example, is the employer asking about your birthplace because there is a concern about your social status or

is it because the interviewer grew up in the same place and is simply trying to make small talk?

Avoid becoming angry, hostile or argumentative. Calmly examine the clumsily expressed question to uncover the underlying concerns of the interviewer. For example, an employer who questions a woman if she is married or about her plans to have children is not really interested in the candidate's personal life but rather is probably attempting to learn how committed the candidate is to the job. You may answer such a question effectively by saying, *"I am assuming by your question that you are concerned with whether or not I will be able to spend the long hours at the office required to get the work done. I'd like to reassure you by mentioning that throughout law school, I held a full-time job, did well in my classes, studied long hours in the library and was not held back in any way by child care responsibilities."*

Thank-you Notes

It is necessary and appropriate to send a thank-you note shortly after an interview. Avoid e-mails. They do not get noticed as quickly and they do not illustrate that you have put much effort into saying thank you. Because this is a business correspondence, send a typed letter, not a handwritten note.

Your letter should be crafted not only to thank people for the time they spent with you and the information they provided but also to restate your interest and clarify any pertinent information you want the employer to remember. Your letter should be structured to affirm that you:

a) paid attention to what was said;
b) understood the interviewer's concerns;
c) are excited about the job; that you can and want to do it;
d) can contribute to the organization immediately.

Some general guidelines for writing strong thank-you letters include:

- Use correct grammar, good sentence structure and standard business letter format.
- Pinpoint how your skills and experience relate to the particular needs of the employer as described during the interview. Focus on what you can do for the employer (what credentials, skills and experience you have that would help the employer), not what the job would do for you.

- Be objective when describing yourself to an employer. For example, instead of writing "I am a hard worker," "I would be a great asset to your firm" or "I have many leadership qualities," show them by means of examples from your past: "The experience I gained as lead counsel of a multimillion dollar deal is indicative of my leadership abilities."
- Limit your thank-you letter to three or four paragraphs. It should rarely be more than one page.
- Close your letter affirming your interest/enthusiasm for the position.

If you interviewed with more than one person, you have two options. You could send a thank-you note to each person; however, do not send three or four people the exact same letter. You ought to vary the letters to reflect a specific aspect of the conversation you had with each individual person.

The second option would be to send one letter to either the most senior person or the person with whom you established the greatest rapport. In your letter, ask that person to extend your thanks to the other individuals (refer to them by name).

Maintain a Follow-up Mindset

Try to avoid the temptation of interpreting what the employer is thinking. Remember, lawyers are trained to not give away cues. Just because you do not hear from the employer the next day or even the next week, do not assume a rejection will follow. Selecting candidates is a slow, time-consuming process. While two weeks on your end of the telephone seems like an eternity, that same timeframe flies by in a flash for an employer. If three or four weeks go past and you have not heard from the employer, call to "check on the status" of your application and reaffirm your interest and enthusiasm for the position.

Summary

Do yourself—and the employer—a favor: Interview as if everything depended on you. Walk in with a clear idea of two or three selling points you would like to express. Use the interviewer's questions to introduce those points and back them up with real-life examples. At the end of the interview, summarize your qualifications and articulate your interest and enthusiasm for the job. If you leave the interview having convinced the employer you have something to offer, nothing—not your color, sex, age, handicap, sexual preference, nationality, etc.—will not stand in your way of landing the job that you want. Take as much control of the follow-up process as you can. Be sure to act in a professional manner; project an image of confidence and dependability and you can't go wrong.

CHAPTER TEN

Kick the Tires and Look Under the Hood

Evaluate and Negotiate Offers

The interviewing process starts with the employer buying and you selling. But, as you get further along in the process, the balance begins to shift. Once an employer has decided to make an offer to you, that employer is then in a position of selling the job to you. That is why the longer you can postpone the salary discussion the more advantageous your position will be.

Some lawyers have unrealistic salary expectations and exaggerated notions of their worth to prospective employers. At the other end of the spectrum are those anxious job seekers who assume that by putting a low price on their skills they will stand a better chance of getting a job offer. If you don't think you are worth much, neither will an employer. Grounded in your knowledge of the market value of the position and your ultimate knowledge of your quality, you should develop a preliminary plan. You need to be able to articulate what you want **specifically**. Break down your financial and non-pecuniary needs into three categories:

> It would be GREAT to have . . .
> I would LIKE to have . . .
> I MUST have . . .

To help you focus, review the section on Values and Career Cores in Chapter Two. Work through "what if" scenarios. Anticipate compromises and plan exactly how far you are willing to scale back on your needs. When a definite salary offer is made, consider it for several moments before you respond. It is now time to negotiate.

Learn to Negotiate

The prospective employer wants to pay a minimum salary to hire a quality employee, which appears to be at odds with your goal of wanting to earn as much as possible. Avoid the trap of viewing negotiating as an adversarial process with winners and losers. Think of it instead as individuals working together to arrive at a mutually beneficial agreement. It is more than trading with others for the things you want. It is discovering ways you can work together to produce positive results for everyone involved. By using sound business principles such as preparing and rehearsing, emphasizing accomplishments rather than personal needs, learning and addressing the needs of the employer, asking intelligent questions and listening carefully, your stature is bound to grow, along with your negotiating leverage. Your approach should always be employer-centered, not self-centered. You must be able to describe your worth in relation to the position that has already been defined. Employers do not care that you have been unemployed for seven months; they do not care that you have $80,000 in school loans, or that you have a mortgage and two children in college. Those facts do not increase your **worth**.

Most people hate the thought of negotiating. But the reality is that if you do not negotiate up front, you may be underpaid by several thousands of dollars over the years. The compensation package you draw at one organization can set the pattern for the level of income you can command when negotiating with another employer. Thus, the terms you agree on will have a far-reaching impact on your entire career. It is not unusual for the difference between the earnings of two individuals to have far less to do with skills and talents than with each person's ability to negotiate.

A general rule of thumb regarding the discussion of compensation is **never to bring up the subject until an offer of employment has been made**. The goal is to give yourself and the interviewer a chance to get to know one another. That way both of you will have a better idea of how flexible you are willing to be with compensation negotiations. You want to ensure that you acquire enough information about the job so that you will be able to effectively communicate that you possess the necessary qualifications for the position. Your goal is to get the employer to invest enough time in you so that you can illustrate that you:

- have done your research on the firm or organization;
- expect to receive compensation appropriate for your level of qualifications and experience;

- want to be compensated on the basis of performance, not on past salary history.

The last point is particularly important. In other disciplines, salary history can illustrate whether a candidate is moving up, across, or down the corporate ladder. In such disciplines, salary can provide some gauge for level of expertise, or it can explain frequent job changes. But because the wide disparity of salary ranges within the legal field is often based on something other than individual performance, salary history actually reveals very little. The reality is that employers do not really care how much money you make. What they really want to know is whether you have realistic expectations about what a job pays. So, always redirect an employer's inquiry about your salary *history* to a focus instead on your salary *requirements*.

Understand that before interviewing candidates employers have established a *predetermined budget* in their minds for the salary that they would like to pay. This figure, of course, is most financially beneficial for the employer. Most employers have some flexibility to negotiate salary, particularly for higher level positions, but, contrary to popular belief, everything is **not** negotiable. Many employers have rigid pay systems—particularly government agencies and corporations but also law firms that use the lockstep model of compensation. These firms try to keep salaries equitable within the organization by not paying anyone much above the norm. As the interview process progresses, the employer **may** consider altering the budget if impressed by the special skills or background of a particular candidate.

It may be at this point that you are asked what your salary expectations are, but be prepared because the salary question can crop up at any time during the job hunt, and it can come in many forms:

- "What is your current salary?"
- "How much were you paid at your previous employer?"
- "What are your salary requirements?"
- "What is the lowest figure you would accept?"
- "How much do you think you are worth?"
- "Why should we pay you more than other fifth-year associates?"

You must be prepared to discuss the salary question whenever the **employer** raises the issue. (But remember, **YOU** should never ask about the salary until you are offered the job.) Be careful. If you state a figure outside of the range the employer has in mind—either too high or too low—you risk having salary used against you as an easy, objective screening device. That is why research during the early stages of your job hunt is so crucial.

Should the salary question arise early in the interview process and you feel you do not have enough information about the position, try to deflect the question:

- "I am unclear about the responsibilities of the position. Could you tell me a little more about…?"
- "I'm looking for a fair market value for the responsibilities involved. I'd like to discuss that when I know a little more about what will be required and you know a little more about what I have to offer you."
- "My interest is in a complete picture. Salary is just one piece of the puzzle. Professional challenge, growth opportunities, benefits, work environment, and relocation are others that will influence my choice. For the right position and company I'm confident we can come to terms. What about xxxxx?" (Redirect the discussion.)
- Or, if said with good-natured humor, you might be effective by asking, "Are we starting negotiations? Do you have an offer in mind?"

Be careful when using humor. If you use the wrong tone or body language, intended humor could come across as obnoxious.

Another technique you could try is to turn the table:

- "Do you have a range in mind, and, if so, would you mind telling me what that is?"
- "What is the normal range in your organization for a position such as this?"
- "What would the range be for someone with my qualifications?"

By getting the employer to state a range first, you can then place the top of this range into the bottom of yours. For example, if the employer's range is $80,000-$100,000, your range should be $100,000-$120,000. Be prepared to articulate why you are worth the salary you are seeking.

If you cannot get the employer to reveal a figure first, try saying:

- "From my research I learned that the range for fourth-year associates in this city is _____. Does this fit your expectation?" (Or, "Is this the range you were considering?")

Notice this has nothing to do with what you are making now. Rather, it focuses the employers on the requirements of the position and on what a fair market value is for equivalent work. If there is an obvious gap between the ranges and your salary expectations, don't simply end the conversation. Go back to criteria and get off of the subject of salary. Try something like:

- "Maybe I didn't understand the requirements of the job. (Restate your understanding of the position.) Is that a fair description of this position, and are there other requirements? From what you have told me about your needs, I was thinking my skills and background in xxxx and yyyy (pick something that emphasizes the unique contributions and spin you would bring to the job) would be an asset, do you agree? Also, based on my research I learned that the range for such a position with your competitors would be..."

Emphasize the level of skill and talent you bring to the table by citing achievements and using statistics, comparisons, and even testimonials to support your case. In other words, **state your value**. You need to explain why the employer will benefit by paying you more money than the predetermined budget.

In the private sector, follow the rule of thirds. Your salary should be approximately one third of the revenue you generate. In order to calculate that, you will need to ask the employer what your expected billing rate would be and how many billable hours are expected. Then do the math.

$$\frac{\text{Your Billing Rate x Number of Required Billable Hours}}{3} = \text{Your Salary}$$

If your billing rate is $250 per hour and 2000 billable hours are expected, you would generate $450,000. Divide that by three and your salary should be in the ballpark of $150,000.

Work *with* the employer—not *against*—to arrive at mutually beneficial solutions. Discovering what the other side wants is crucial to arriving at satisfactory agreements. Build a strategy that focuses on working out the best agreement for everyone. Seek to understand all dimensions of an issue. Focusing only on your own immediate payoff can have dire consequences, so learn to consider negotiations from everyone's perspective. Remember, the value of what you have to offer depends on the perceptions of the person or people you are negotiating with. To strengthen your negotiating stance, determine what the employer "values" and respond accordingly. It is your responsibility to calmly educate the employer on the "value added" component acquired by hiring you.

It Is All About "Attitude"

You can affect—positively or negatively—the way you are positioned in the minds of those with whom you negotiate by the attitude you project. Confidence is an extremely important asset at this phase of the job hunt. Organize your thoughts. Make sure you can get your main point across in the most concise and compelling way. Process an idea through to its logical conclusion by evaluating the possible responses you may get from the other side. Choose your words carefully. Focus on clarity and precision in your speech. State your position firmly. Carry yourself with confidence, and position yourself as a person with negotiating power.

Be open and honest about what you want, but remember to be careful about how much information you reveal. Think about what information you don't necessarily want employers to have. Keep in mind that an interview is not a therapy session. Tell employers what they need to know or what they ask about. Remember, the more you talk, the more likely you are to sabotage your own efforts—so think through your presentation.

Don't be reticent to ask questions. Skillfully asked questions can transform negotiations from an adversarial conflict into a partnership. By asking questions, you make sure that the employer will talk more and you will talk less. Be careful about the types of questions you ask, and phrase inquiries in positive, non-threatening terms. Start with open-ended questions and move on to narrower, more direct questions. Once you have asked a question, be quiet and *listen* to the response.

Throughout the negotiating process remember to constantly reinforce the perception that you are excited about the offer and that you want to take this position, even if you are disappointed with the figure. You do not want the negotiation to be an argument but rather a way that you can get to the place where you want to be in order to accept the offer. Remember, your strategy is to get to your top figure in a way the employer thinks is fair.

If you are unhappy with what has been offered, it is appropriate to come back with a counteroffer. The key is to emphasize the benefit to the employer of paying you more. Perhaps if the employer cannot meet your salary expectations, you may be able to convince the employer to give you "credit" for judicial clerkships, superior academic performance, past careers or skill sets. Perhaps you can convince the employer to create a new position that would better accommodate your skills, interests, and abilities as well as meeting the employer's needs. If moving to a different specialty or industry, keep in mind the employer may want proof of performance **before** feeling justified in giving you the income you want. Request a review and increase in six months based on your ability to meet a preset goal. Demonstrate your confidence in your abilities by saying something like:

- "Let me prove I am worth this. I would be happy to come in at this salary if you could agree to review my performance in six months."

Even after you are clear about the offer and are pleased with it, it is in your best interest **not** to accept the job just yet. Take time to reflect on what has been agreed upon:

- "This sounds terrific. I'd like to think it over to make sure we haven't missed anything," OR
- "This sounds terrific. I'd like to think it over to make sure we have covered everything. What is your timeframe? When would you like my response?" OR
- "I am very excited about the offer. Can you tell me what your timeframe for a reply is?"

It is common professional courtesy for employers to provide candidates with at least 48 hours to consider an offer.

Leverage Multiple Offers and Counteroffers

If you are waiting to hear from other employers, contact them immediately and let them know you have an offer and would like to clarify your application status before you make any decisions. A second offer in hand could enhance your bargaining power. However, **never** lie about having another offer. While the lie might work, it could backfire and create ill will if the employer ever finds out. When you compromise your integrity, you demean your value to others and to yourself.

You may find your current employer is surprised when you announce that you are leaving and responds with a counteroffer. If you find yourself in this predicament, you may want to ask yourself:

- Why did I interview in the first place? Do I really want to move or am I happy in my current situation?

- Is this counteroffer an indication of my value to the organization or simply a stopgap measure to keep me around until they can find a replacement?
- Should I accept the new opportunity or stay where I have established relationships and a good track record?

Deciding between two offers is anxiety provoking. Review your long-term goals and consider if either position will enable you to reach your goals more quickly or take you in an entirely different direction. What impact will each position have on other parts of your life?

EXERCISE: Evaluating Offers

To help you make your decision, go back to Chapter Two and review the values you ranked "A" and ordered from 1 to 10. List those values on the chart below and give each one a grade of A to F. By comparing the jobs point by point, it will become clear which is the better offer for you.

"A" VALUES	Job #1	Job #2
1.		
2.		
3.		
4.		
5.		
6.		
7.		
8.		
9.		
10.		

Finalize Agreements

Don't leave details hanging. It is often amazing how two people sitting in the same room can have quite different perspectives concerning what was agreed upon. To ensure that everyone is clear, you may want to summarize by saying:

- "So, as I understand it, I will be expected to (restate your understanding of the position) in exchange for (restate the compensation package offered)."

Summary

It is important to know when to stop negotiating and start the job. Reaching common ground and setting the stage for mutual respect and cooperation may be more important than the few extra dollars you might be able to obtain by playing games. Having your priorities in place will help you decide which things you are willing to sacrifice in the negotiating process. Keep the following negotiating tips in mind:

- Find out everything you can before you start to negotiate.
- Design a strategy that focuses on working out the best agreement for everyone.
- Deal fairly and honestly with people.
- Always identify one person within the organization to negotiate with.
- Always get right to the point. Be concise.
- Oversimplify and repeat your message until it sinks in.
- Translate your skills into benefits for the listener.
- Talk about **value** not **cost.**
- State what you want in clear and concise terms and listen for a response.
- Explore all your options. The more options you can generate, the stronger your position.
- Be prepared to explain why something is unacceptable and offer a counter-solution.
- Finalize all details.
- Always be mindful about how this negotiation might affect future relations.

Career Cruise Control

At a certain point in your professional life, you begin to feel confident in your abilities and in control of your environment. We all strive to get to that point in our careers so we can enjoy the fruits of our labor. However, a sure-fire way to derail your career is to assume at that point that you have nothing left to learn and can simply rest on your laurels. Remember, even when you decide to use the cruise control feature in your car, you still must stay alert and keep your eyes on the road and drive defensively.

Master Office Politics

Attorneys must be adept at navigating their way through the quagmire of office politics. Playing office politics conjures up images of the brown-nosing "yes man" willing to sell his soul to get ahead. That is certainly one example; however, it is office politics at its worst. At its best, office politics simply is a cultural assessment of the employer; it is acknowledging how to accomplish things within your organization. Understanding the politics can mean the difference between a mediocre career and a quick rise to stardom. So, whether your goal is to some day rule the office or simply to get the best assignments, training, experience and exposure, it is imperative to understand the political landscape.

First, pay attention to the rules. Knowing the rules will save you from potentially embarrassing, career-altering goofs from which it might be difficult to recover. The written rules will explain things like time off to which you are entitled, reimbursable expenses; perks and benefits as well as established procedures for photocopying, proofreading, requesting additional support services, etc. Review Employee Handbooks and other manuals you received when you first joined the organization to familiarize yourself with such information.

The unspoken/unwritten rules are even more important though some-times less obvious to discern. However, simple observation can uncover mountains of information. For example, observation can reveal how man-agement reacts to employees who take all the time off to which the written rules say they are entitled; it may reveal that department leaders begin work at 8:00 a.m. each day and NOT 9:00 a.m. as the written policy states. Careful observation can also uncover *true* billable requirements. While 1900 hours may be the stated requirement, you may find that associates labeled "successful" bill closer to 2100 hours. Armed with all this information, you can determine what you need to do to advance your career within the orga-nization. It would behoove you to pay attention.

In addition to knowing the rules, you want to be in the information loop. Listen to rumors and gossip. Don't spread it, don't comment on it and don't believe it is 100% accurate, but know it. Knowing the reputa-tions of organization leaders will help you uncover not only who the politi-cally powerful players are but also what skill sets are rewarded in this cul-ture. If your long-term goal is to be a leader at this organization, note the common attributes the leaders posses and think about ways to begin to develop similar attributes. Listen to the gossip to uncover the reputations of your peers and colleagues. Who have been labeled "superstars," "losers" and "troublemakers?" What characteristics do they have in common? Do you share any of these characteristics? Can you emulate the positive char-acteristics? Can you shed the negative ones? Again, pay attention.

Read the brochures and literature your organization distributes to cli-ents and new recruits. These documents shed light on institutional values, cultures and norms. Know as much about your organization as possible throughout your tenure there. Remember, information is power.

It is important to understand power. At every organization, there are two kinds of power: "Position Power" and "Personal Power." *Position Power* is based on a person's role within the organization: department manager, committee chair, etc., while *Personal Power* is your innate ability to accom-plish tasks and goals no matter where you are on the food chain. Career advancement is based on your ability to master your personal power. To do so, you must understand the golden rule: People want to work with those they can rely on to do quality work in a timely fashion. By developing a reputation as the "go to" person who happily performs the less desirable assignments with the same level of enthusiasm and attention to detail as the "sexy" assignments, you will be sought after by the powers-that-be because you make their lives easier.

Take care of your reputation. Protect your character. Let people know who you are and what you can do. Benchmark your progress against your colleagues. If others appear to be getting more sophisticated work, ask yourself why. Is it because you have not proven yourself to be reliable? Is your substantive work not up to par? Answers to these questions can help you see yourself through the eyes of your superiors and enable you to address issues before they become monumental. And, before you assume there is some great conspiracy by the power structure to sabotage your career, determine how your behavior may be contributing to the situation and try to correct that first.

EXERCISE: Annual Self-Appraisal

Each year, BEFORE your formal evaluation, take stock of your own performance.

1. List the clients for whom I did a substantial amount of work or the major projects I worked on.

2. List significant accomplishments for the past year.

3. Is my workload insufficient, satisfactory, or too much?

4. Am I receiving a sufficient variety of assignments to enable me to grow as a lawyer? If not, what can I do to address the issue?

5. List any knowledge, skills or abilities not being fully utilized in my assignments. Describe how they might be used better.

6. Have I had regular opportunities to discuss my work with supervisors? If not, what could I have done differently to get needed feedback?

7. Have I received and acted on supervisors' suggestions for improving my work?

8. List internal activities I have participated in that contribute to the organization's mission (i.e., recruiting, committee assignments, CLEs, etc).

9. List professional and community activities of the last twelve months. Include external activities (speaking engagements, articles written, conventions and seminars attended, bar activities, community activities, etc.).

10. What are my goals for the next year? In what areas would I like to improve and what is my action plan to accomplish this?

Consider any difficulties (personal or professional) that may have impeded your performance, but do not put this information in writing. Think about whether or not it would be appropriate to verbally share that information during your view. For example, if tending to a family illness earlier in the year is responsible for lower than expected billable hours, it might be helpful to point that out so your productivity can be viewed in perspective. Carefully consider the information you want to share. And, even if you choose not to share specific information, if there is something impacting your performance, make sure you design a strategy to deal with it before it becomes a bigger issue.

Refer back to the Long-Term Goals and 5-Year Plan you created in Chapter Two to ensure you are staying on course.

Learn to Delegate

Road trips go more smoothly when there are others with whom to share the tasks. The driver can concentrate more effectively when there is someone by his side reading the map and one person in the backseat handing him a bottled water while another naps to prepare for her turn at the wheel.

Delegating is an often overlooked yet essential skill to master. Its purpose is to enable you to dispose of simpler tasks to free you up to perform tasks that are of greater *value* to your organization. The time it takes up front to orchestrate a plan of action, explain the desired outcome and monitor the progress of each subordinate ultimately is less than the time it would take to execute the entire action plan yourself. That is, if you delegate *correctly*.

You hamper your ability to delegate effectively if you:
- believe you can do the task better/faster yourself;
- worry that a subordinate might not do the task properly and, because you are ultimately accountable, your reputation may be at risk;
- fear that if the subordinate does do it well, you may be viewed as "non-essential" or expendable.

The truth is you probably can do the specific task better and faster. However, as you move up the hierarchy in your career, additional responsibilities will also require your attention. With the same amount of hours in each day and multiplying responsibilities, you have to use every available resource to get all the work done. Accept the fact that occasionally it will take more time to explain to someone else how to perform a task than it would take to do it yourself. Delegate it anyway. The next time, it will take less time to explain. More importantly, you will be developing your team for the future and thus ultimately gain the leverage and control you are seeking. And remember, people rise or fall to the level of expectation. Delegate tasks and hold people accountable. The better your team does under your leadership, the more *value* you will bring to your organization. No one ever lost a job for being too productive.

Understand that there is a difference between *assigning* a task and *delegating* one. If there are multiple directives, required check-ins and a significant amount of supervision time, you have merely assigned the task. This method will cause you to become a choke point and slow down the work process. Nothing will render you expendable or non-essential faster than being seen as the bottleneck, responsible for missed deadlines and an underutilized team.

To become a more effective delegator, use the four-step process outlined below. Keep in mind, you can use this model to delegate in your personal life too. Children and spouses can share chores; there are also paid services to do the laundry, mow the lawn or clean the house. Delegating in your personal and professional life will allow you to strike the balance you are seeking.

STEP 1: THINK IT THROUGH.

Every successful project has defined and approved goals, a committed team and a viable plan of action that can effectively accommodate change. Invest the time at the beginning of the project to think through the project. This will enable you to clearly define the goals and objectives, assign the tasks and assess the progress to ensure you get the result you want, which will ultimately save time. Consider:

- What is the goal or desired result?
- How many people do I need to accomplish the goal? What type of skills do they need to possess?
- Can some of the tasks be carried out in parallel?
- Will delegating critical tasks to someone else free me up to troubleshoot as problems arise without delaying the project?
- Are there competing projects with higher priorities that are going to take up key resources?

STEP 2: ASSEMBLE THE TEAM

Identify the person(s) who can get the job done. (Granted, sometimes you have no choice of team members. In that instance, the next steps are even more critical.) Be sure to get a commitment from each team member that they:

- have the ability to perform the task;
- understand the project's overall objective;
- can complete the task in the allotted timeframe;
- are aware of established performance standards.

STEP 3: IMPLEMENT THE ACTION PLAN

Once you know who is on the team and have a sense of their strengths and weaknesses, you will want to decide which of the six levels of delegation is appropriate for their skill level and your comfort level. Be clear about the delegation level at which your subordinate is expected to operate.

1. **Research and Report**: subordinate is asked to research specific information and report back on findings;
2. **Recommend Action**: subordinate is asked to research specific information, formulate multiple suggestions as to how to proceed, and come back to discuss;
3. **Take Action—When I say GO**: subordinate is expected to check in with you before acting;
4. **Take Action—Unless I say NO**; subordinate is expected to take action unless you step in and say not to;
5. **Take Action and Let me know what you did**: subordinate takes ownership of projects and is expected to keep you in the loop;

6. **Take Action and I don't want to hear about it again:** subordinate operates independently.

As you work more and more with people and trust develops, you will get more comfortable delegating at higher levels.

STEP 4: COMMUNICATE. COMMUNICATE. COMMUNICATE

Always operate under the principle that you can never be too clear. As the delegator, it is your responsibility to ensure your subordinates know:

- Goals and Objectives of the Project. Too many busy professionals delegate under the command and control style of "Do this because I said so." They believe it will take too long to explain the details. However, if everybody understands the overall objective (which typically can be explained in 3 sentences in less than 30 seconds) or how their segment of the project ties into the overall goal, they will be more invested in the project and better serve the needs of the organization.

- Operating Procedures. Let people know how information will be shared (e-mail, voicemail, meetings, etc.), who else is working on the project and any other peculiarities specific to this project.

- SPECIFIC Deadlines. "ASAP" is meaningless. So is "In a few days." Try, "I need it in an hour" or "I need it Wednesday afternoon." Leave no room for ambiguity. Setting specific deadlines and allowing your team to manage its own workload will ameliorate your constant need to hover and inquire "is it done yet?" to the relief of both you and your team members.

- Expected Performance Standards. Even if you believe people should know what is expected of them—take the 10 seconds required to state the obvious. Remember, you can never be too clear.

- How They Are Doing Along the Way. Provide on-going feedback to allow for corrections to be made as the project progresses.

Delegating is not just a way to reduce your workload and complete projects. It is a way to develop employees and strengthen the workforce.

Once you learn to mobilize forces around you, you will maximize your leverage, free yourself up to perform tasks of greater value to your organization and maybe even find a little spare time to enjoy your life.

Summary

No matter how senior you are; no matter how competent you have become, NEVER assume there is nothing else to learn or no additional tasks to master. Your success—however you have defined it—requires you to constantly reassess your abilities and values; it requires you to monitor needed course corrections to achieve short- and long-term goals; and it requires you to stay connected to people who can help you.

Keep your eyes on the road, maintain your vehicle and enjoy the journey.

Career Advice From Those in the Know

As I was writing **Navigating Detours on the Road to Success: A Lawyer's Guide to Career Management,** I reached out to mentors, colleagues and attorneys in my own network and asked them to complete the sentence:

"The best piece of career advice I ever got was..."

Take heed of these wonderful pearls of wisdom.

"The best piece of advice I ever got was from Lou Jackson who said: 'talk to the guy; talk to the gal.'"

"The second best piece of career advice I ever got was from my partner Pat Vaccaro who said, 'everything you do you do for reputation.'"

- William Krupman
Managing Partner, Jackson Lewis

"Never say you can't work the weekend because you have to play in a golf tournament."

- Charles Capetanakis
Partner, Capetankis & Preite

"Always dress for the job you want to have, not the job you have."
- Lauren D. Ruff
Associate, Willkie Farr & Gallagher

"I remember a college law professor advising me that law school would be a good option since there are so many things you can do with a law degree. And be nice to secretaries."

- James Doherty
Associate, Eisenberg, Tanchum & Levy

Reilly's Law: "Bodies in motion will remain in motion; Bodies at rest will definitely remain at rest."

- Robert Reilly

Assistant Dean, Fordham University School of Law

"Don't make stupid mistakes because once you are known as Joe Jerk you will always be known as Joe Jerk no matter how much you improve."

- Matthew Jeon

Partner, Jeon & Kim

"When God closes a door, somewhere He opens a window."

- Reverend Mother, *Sound of Music*

"The firm isn't going to make you successful, you are going to make yourself, and thereby the firm, successful. You have to go out and find the opportunities for growth and development."

- Jay Sullivan

Partner, Exec|Comm

"Whenever an issue is raised, at a minimum have the documents and the facts but also try to have an answer, a solution or alternative proposals before you take an issue to a senior attorney or partner."

- Deirdre Sullivan

Associate, Milbank, Tweed, Hadley & McCloy LLC

"Best piece of legal advice I ever received was from my great friend Ed Campbell…he told me that when you talk to anyone assume they are wired and the tape will one day be played back in court…if you keep this in mind you will never get in trouble…he was right…thirty years practicing law."

- James Martorano

Legal Aid Society

"Be sure that you understand each assignment and don't be afraid to seek clarification. Better to ask a few more questions than to invest hours (perhaps billable) going off on a tangent and producing a product that no one can use."

- Judy Mender

Assistant Dean, Benjamin Cardozo School of Law

"Remember when attending a meeting, on a telephone call, or in court, that what is **not** *said is often more important than what is said."*

\- Denis Cronin

Partner, Cronin & Vris LLP

"If one advances confidently in the direction of his dreams and endeavors to live the life which he has imagined, he will meet with a success unexpected in common hours."

\- Thoreau

"Here are three pearls of wisdom: 1) it's not who you know but who knows you; 2) you are your own best bet; and 3) you choose to do these things. The first statement came from my house cleaner; the second came from a patent lawyer when I was contemplating starting my own business and the third came from my ten-year old son. Specifically, I was driving and complaining about all of the things that I do for others that go unrecognized and unappreciated. He looked at me, didn't even flinch; not even a blink of the eye and stated blankly "you choose to do these things." He was right. As a result, I've delegated a great deal of tasks so that I can focus on number one: me!

\- Katherine Frink-Hamlett

President, Frink-Hamlett

"There is no such thing as a safe, completely secure job. Your security lies within. The most important thing is to know what you are best at, what your skills are, and how they can help a potential employer. If you know your best skills and can translate them to an employer to meet a need that he or she has, you will have job security."

\- Wendy L. Werner

Werner Associates

"Your career is really your own responsibility and you cannot look to an employer to manage it for you."

\- Patricia Stacey

Director of Legal Hiring, Duane Morris LLP

"Do what you love and it will never truly feel like work, it will feel like life. This was the best advice I received and though it did not make me wealthy, it kept me happy, healthy and wise."

\- Jodi Greenspan

Assistant Dean Career Services

Loyola University School of Law - Chicago

"The best piece of career advice I ever got was from a Senior Partner who told me to make sure to eat lunch, eat dinner and stay home when sick, because no one else is going to take care of your health. If you are not healthy and your mind is not sharp, you are no good to the firm and no good to the clients "

- Jean Marie Campbell

Firmwide Director of Attorney Development

Akin Gump Strauss Hauer & Feld LLP

"The best piece of career advice I ever had came from my first supervisor who told me never to discount those things that you are good at that come easy to you. During an annual performance review I had discounted my skills in a particular part of my job since they came to me naturally and didn't really feel like work…he pointed out that when you find that 'something' that you like to do, that you're good at and that others value—you've struck the mother lode."

- Fred Thrasher

Deputy Director

NALP

"The best piece of career advice I ever got was from my father, when I was going to college. I was enrolling in a small liberal arts program at a major public university, and he recommended that I take at least 2 entry-level accounting classes (financial and managerial) in the business school. Those classes gave me an advantage in my first job out of college, in a litigation and bankruptcy consulting group at a Big 6 accounting firm, and also in my career in corporate law, where I read countless financial statements and worked closely with issuers' accountants."

- Emily Campbell

Laura Seigal & Associates

"Those who talk don't know; and those who know don't talk. Of course that's not an absolute rule, but I tend to be reflective in the 'grain of salt' application."

- John Mastandra

Director, On-Line Division

Practicing Law Institute

"While I don't profess to be in the know, I offer two completions:
1. It is very hard to learn anything while you're talking.
2. Treat court clerks and court officers as judges".

- Michael Stanton

Partner, Weil Gotshal & Manges

"Don't burn any bridges."

\- Jill Kirson

U.S. Securities and Exchange Committee

"The best piece of career advice that I ever received was to work hard, ignore the petty competitive concerns of others, and to conduct myself with honor and integrity at all times. I've followed the blueprint and it has worked well for me professionally. It's also allowed me to sleep easily. Another pearl was that when dealing with an unexpected group split, the ultimate best offer (assuming that you're wanted by both parties) will come from your present team. That held true for me as well."

\- Kristopher Hansen

Partner, Stroock and Stroock and Lavan

"On slow days, smile and dial. Very effective business development tool, you know."

\- Luis Palacios

Associate, Rodrigo, Elias & Merdrano

"When a classmate said, 'Make an appointment to talk to Kathy Brady, she's great.'

\- Robert Holdman

Assistant District Attorney, Bronx D.A.

Selected Web Resources

SEARCH ENGINES

www.google.com

www.askjeeves.com

www.alltheweb.com

www.altavista.com

www.ask.com

JOB BOARDS

Legal

www.emplawyernet.com

www.careers. Findlaw.com

www.findlawjob.com

www.legalstaff.com

www.amlawjobs.com

www.attorneyjobs.com

http://lawjob.com

www.legaldreamjobs.com

www.lawyersweekly.com

www.lawcrossings.com

General

www.upladder.com

www.careers.wsj.com

www.netshare.com

www.hotjobs.com

www.careerbuilder.com

www.monsterboard.com

www.craigslist.org

www.ajb.dni.us/ *(America's Job Bank)*

www.bestjobusa.com

www.coolworks.com

www.directemployers.com

Specialty

www.adr.org *(American Arbitration Association)*

www.experienceworks.org *(specializes in placing seniors)*

www.chronicle.edu *(Chronicle of Higher Education)*

www.jobline.acca.com *(American Corporate Counsel Association)*

www.jobsforrecruiters.com *(Legal Administration)*

www.pslawnet.org *(Public Interest Jobs)*

www.unsystem.org or www.un.org/depts/OHRM/indexpo.htm *(United Nations Systems)*

www.philanthropy-journal.org *(Philanthropy)*

www.elfnetwork.com *(Non-profit jobs)*

www.humanrightsjobs.com

www.idealist.org *(Non-profit)*

www.opajobs.com *(Public Relations/Government Affairs)*

www.naag.org *(National Association of Attorneys General)*

www.ndaa-apri.org *(National District Attorneys Association)*

www.nlada.org/jobop.htm *(National Legal Aid and Defender Association)*

Public Service

www.usajobs.opm.gov *(US Office of Personnel Management)*

www.alldc.org *(Lobbying jobs)*

www.access.gpo.gov/plumbook

www.job-hunt.org

www.rollcall.com

www.hillzoo.com

www.opensecrets.org

www.fedworld.gov

www.usdoj.gov

www.probono.net

Recruiters

www.nalsc.org *(National Association of Legal Search Consultants)*

www.findarecruiter.com

www.executivejobsusa.com

www.strategicworkforce.com *(temp and temp to perm)*

www.peakorg.com

www.specialcounsel.com

RESEARCH RESOURCES

http://abbott-langer.com

http://bls.gov

www.worldatwork.org

www.workforce.com

www.vault.com

www.hildebrandt.com

www.altmanweil.com

www.legalauthority.com

www.ioma.com

www.martindale.com

www.nalp.org

www.nalpdirectory.com/

www.shrm.org

www.ceoexpress.com

www.hoovers.com

www.lawguru.com

www.anywho.com

http://attorneys.com

www.celesq.com

www.yahoo.com/business_and_economy/

www.jobsmart.org

www.infirmation.com

RELOCATION/SALARY

www.payscale.com

www.salary.com

www.law360.com

www.rpsrelocation.com

BAR ASSOCIATIONS

www.findlaw.com/06association/index.html

www.courts.state.us

www.abanet.org *(American Bar Association)*

www.hnba.com *(Hispanic National Bar Association)*

www.napil.org *(National Association for Public Interest Law)*

www.nationalbar.org *(African American Bar Association)*

www.napaba.org *(National Asian Pacific American Association)*

www.nlgla.org *(National Lesbian and Gay Law Association)*

DIVERSITY

www.worklifecongress.com

www.diversitylink.com

www.workoptions.com

BAR ASSOCIATIONS

www.keirsey.com

www.od-online.com

www.platinumrule.com

www.self-directed-search.com *($8.95)*

www.careerkey.org

- breadth to depth
- developmt has hit a well due to small size
- need to grow, larger corp

Jams - very busy

NASDAQ NYSE - Empl. Arbitrali..
            Sports - employmt
        have staff

- Empl Adjuncts at Fordh..

- Clerkship?

- Fordham · Adriezi

- Wrkg Women Top 100 Corps
        - search the webs of these cos.

Covidien - 250 plus 30% bonus · stock options
        · work on "What is your comp now?" response
        · 2 Assoc GC · 2 person reporting
        · Respiratory Support "line" "Corporate"
legal dept (not IP) rep-ng to GC Paul
litigation, m+a due dili., mng contracts negoti..
        · will call in Zukes - calendar Co. To deep
        · Ralph Blessini, Mark Feg... Mana Legal
        8.2.

ca? bok on website

Printed in the United States
207608BV00003B/31-129/A